I don't know about you, b
life. Sins, sufferings, sorrows ~~just to name a few. In *10 Women*~~
Who Overcame Their Past, Dayspring MacLeod introduces us
to women throughout Christian history who faced difficult
circumstances, painful hardships, and enslaving sins. Through
these stories, we see women who overcame, but not in their
own power and strength; rather, through the redemptive work
of Christ on their behalf. In reading *10 Women*, you'll meet
sisters in Christ whose lives and testimony both encourage
and equip you to turn to Christ, the author and perfecter of
your faith.

Christina Fox
Author of *A Heart Set Free: A Journey to Hope Through the Psalms
of Lament* and *Tell God How You Feel.*

We all face challenges. We must navigate them without letting
them define us and walk by faith as we trust in our sovereign
Lord. That's easier said than done. Clearly, some challenges
seem overwhelming. *10 Women Who Overcame Their Past* is
a thought-provoking read that introduces ten very different
women with ten very different struggles, who serve the same
Lord who is at work in every situation to bring glory to
Himself. As readers think through the myriad of issues tackled
here, Dayspring MacLeod asks and answers the question of
whether fruit can be harvested. Praise God, it can be. What
an encouragement that is for us all.

Mary K. Mohler
Author, *Growing in Gratitude*
Director, Seminary Wives Institute

How many of us wonder about the usefulness of our suffering? *Can God really redeem it*, we ask? Dayspring helps us see the biblical answer, which is YES. In Christ, we are loved, sought after, purchased, and brought into a family legacy that can never be broken—even when we feel broken and crushed by our circumstances. You'll want to read *10 Women Who Overcame Their Past* and rejoice in our redeeming, victorious Lord and Savior, whose yoke is easy and whose burden is light.

Kristen Wetherell
Author of *Humble Moms, Fight Your Fears*, and co-author of
Hope When It Hurts

10
WOMEN WHO OVERCAME THEIR PAST

❖

Dayspring MacLeod

CHRISTIAN
FOCUS

Contents

For Flòraidh, when the going gets hard: to help you walk with the One who truly overcomes.

Foreword

Young people growing up are intensely aware of the real world around them. Sometimes the adults in their lives close their eyes to this truth but, thankfully, Dayspring MacLeod, who wrote this book, does not. Using the stories of Christian women past and present she tackles the hard subjects that confront young adults in the media, in school and college, in their friendship groups and, yes, in their churches too.

Relationships can be a minefield, from sexual identity to failed marriages, from sudden widowhood to the challenges of singleness. As each subject is tackled the reader discovers that it's alright to ask hard questions. The Bible doesn't run away from reality and neither should Christians. These issues are explored through the lens of the Bible.

There are complexities in life other than relationships, forgiveness, eating disorders and illness among them. The book provides no easy answers, but it shows how, in the real lives of real women, ways are found through the problems that present themselves to believers and how God is faithful to His promises even in the darkest of days.

The potent trio of false beliefs, self-righteousness and the fear of man complete the book. Once again, the lives of women who, through the centuries, have faced these issues are used to show today's women that they are not alone, that others are there for them and that God will not fail.

Each chapter ends by asking 'can I bear fruit?', with a set of questions to consider. The answer to the first question is a reassuring 'yes'. And the final questions will keep the reader and her friends deep in conversation for some time.

Having spent some years writing the *Ten Girls / Ten Boys Lightkeepers* series of books for younger children it gladdens my heart to see Dayspring MacLeod reaching out for the baton and running with it by writing for adults. I was privileged to read her early efforts at writing and encourage her on her way. I'm so glad I did!

Irene Howat
September 2021

Introduction

If you were to think of one woman from the Bible as a template for overcoming her past, who would it be? Some of the first names to come to mind might be Rahab (once a prostitute; became a pillar of the early nation of Israel), Mary Magdalene (demon possession), Mary the mother of Jesus (the scandal of unwed pregnancy), or the Woman at the Well (serial monogamy). But as I started thinking about the women of the Bible, a much greater variety of 'bad pasts' emerged. Sarah was a control freak. Rebekah practiced extreme favouritism of her children. Leah suffered ongoing rejection. Hannah experienced infertility and bullying. Abigail had a terrible marriage. Miriam impatiently grasped for authority herself instead of recognising God's slower work through her brother. Esther emerged from a childhood of orphanhood, poverty, and being ruled by fear.

But of all the 'bad pasts' in the Bible, the one that I found most thought-provoking was Naomi's. Naomi's 'bad past' wasn't something she carried through her whole life. She wasn't born into slavery or forced into prostitution at a young age. Her big trial didn't start until she was an established wife and mother. But when it started, boy, did she suffer. She saw the terrifying ravages of

She lost hope and faith, believing she could never see God's favour again.

famine in her own country; she became a refugee; she (along with her husband) made bad choices regarding their family, particularly having their children marry outside the faith; her husband and both sons died far from home. This last event is what triggered Naomi's bitterness. It was so all-consuming that she made it her identity, insisting on being called Mara (bitter). She used it to push away anyone who claimed to still love her. She lost hope and faith, believing she could never see God's favour again.[1]

Naomi could never have clawed her way back into joy in God's presence. It was only through His outrageous pursuit of her, His manifestation of care for her through the patient servanthood of her daughter-in-law and the glorious provision of Boaz, that Naomi was able to recognise that bitterness was not who she was. Did that mean she put the deaths of her loved ones, and all the trauma of refugeehood and stepping outside of God's law, behind her? The grief no doubt remained all her life, along with the regretful knowledge of ways in which she had harmed herself and her family. But when God reminded her that He still had a future for her, she was able to step outside of her despair and be His joyful servant again. From

1   Told in the Book of Ruth.

our vantage point in history, we know what Naomi didn't even see in her lifetime: that His blessing of her family didn't stop there, but blossomed into the birth of King David only two generations later, and ultimately into the birth of Christ. God had used Mara, 'Bitter', to bring into His family a foreign widow who would have a place in the lineage of the Messiah. Now that is something so outrageous only God could conceive of it!

You may have made mistakes in your life, and may have known terrible circumstances. You may still be in the midst of a trial; you

your future is both certain and bright.

may even feel defined by it. But know this – that God is not constrained by your definition, your identity, your feelings of uselessness or failure or victimhood. And He doesn't want you to be either. If you know Jesus, you are His hard-won inheritance, His spotless bride, and your future is both certain and bright. He wants you to leave your sins, your failures and your traumas with Him, so that you can be free to serve. He wants to make your yoke easy, bearing the weight of it Himself, while you remain harnessed to Him, keeping in step and close to His side.

You may have years – perhaps many of them – that the locusts have eaten. Jesus has the power to change them into a legacy of His grace, such that you remember the worst times with joy as you see how He worked through them. Through exploring how other women of Christ's kingdom began anew in Him, you will be encouraged on your own path of joy and freedom. You will learn how to allow God to do His work in you during the precious times of testing, instead of resisting both the suffering and the lessons. You will learn to trust Him more, to hold Him ever dearer, and to bring your burdens to Him. You will see that you are precious and beloved and without stain or blemish before the Holy One. To those who are struggling, I want to encourage you to tell these truths to yourself over and over again, especially using Scriptures, which have infinite power to knock back the lies of Satan which whisper that the past will always drag you down. Victory, freedom, abundant life, fruitfulness – these are all still yours.

First, a brief note on who will benefit from this book. You may turn initially to the subject which speaks loudest into your own situation, but I do believe there is something for every Christian woman in each chapter. You may not be same-sex attracted like Rosaria Butterfield, but you have certainly fought against sexual temptation; you may not have battled an eating disorder like Christie Dondero Bettwy, but you have probably desired control in unhealthy ways. We have all contended with our sin natures, and each woman's story is applicable to these wider issues. As far as possible, I have let these women tell their stories in their own words. Let's learn together as we explore the stories of our sisters in Christ.

1 Sexual Sin & Identity

Dr Rosaria Champagne Butterfield

Who am I?

We all have a story to tell ourselves about who we are, and it usually starts with where we come from, which people we 'belong' to, and what our occupation is.

I am a thirty-something American woman living in Scotland. I am a wife, mother of three, and a writer. This tells you about my place in society, and in relation to those closest to me. It orients me in terms of my sense of community. If we delve a bit further, we might come up with: *I am interested in politics but politically homeless, a history and literature buff, and a major musical theatre fan. Memes cheer me up on a bad day; I will never say no to chocolate or yes to fruit salad; and my most treasured possessions are Christmas ornaments.*

My identity is the part of me I introduce to strangers – the basic facts that show them how they might relate to me. My personality is what people discover as they get to know me: the parts we guard as vulnerable, as lovable or unlovable, acceptable or unacceptable.

We live in a uniquely introspective and individualistic society which spends a great deal of time considering how we define ourselves and whom we identify with. One of the faultlines that has emerged most closely in this evolution is our sexual identity; and one of the most influential thinkers on this topic in the twenty-first-century Church is Dr Rosaria Butterfield. In the 1990s, Dr Butterfield was a professor of English at Syracuse University, where she was also active in the lesbian and feminist communities. In her second book, *Openness Unhindered*, she summarises her journey from finding her identity in her gender and sexuality to finding herself defined 'in Christ'.

In Her Own Words

From the age of twenty-two until twenty-eight, I continued to date men and at the same time feel a sense of longing and connection that toppled over the edges for my women friends, especially my friends from my growing lesbian and feminist community base.

I never hated men. They just didn't show up on my radar in ways as meaningful, deep or important. I never dreamed of marriage or kids. I presumed that I was straight. Men like me. I tolerated sexual advances. And I remained steadfastly curious about what it would be like to be with a woman.

This repetitious lesbian sensibility rooted and grew: I simply preferred the company of women. In my late twenties, enhanced by feminist philosophy and LGBT political advocacy, my homosocial preference morphed into homosexuality. That shift was subtle, not startling. My lesbian identity and my love for my LGBT community developed in sync with my lesbian sexual practice. Life finally came together for me and made sense.

My life as a lesbian seemed normal. I considered it an enlightened, chosen path. Lesbianism felt like a cleaner and more moral sexual practice. Always preferring symmetry to asymmetry, I believed I had found my real self. Many other women in my lesbian community had had a heterosexual season. We believed that was because heterosexuality had become, in the words of the late lesbian poet and English professor Adrienne Rich, compulsory. When I fell in love with a woman for the first time, I thought I had found my real self. I was hooked, and I had no intention of looking back.

What happened to my Catholic training? I believed now that faith in God was superstitious and intellectually untenable.

The name Jesus, which had rolled off my tongue in a little girl's prayers, then rolled off my back in college, now made me recoil with anger.

My next lesbian partner and I shared many vital interests: AIDS activism, children's health and literacy, golden retriever rescue, and our Unitarian Universalist church, to name a few. It was hard to argue that she and I were anything but good citizens and caregivers. The LGBT community values hospitality and applies it with skill, sacrifice and integrity. Indeed, I honed the hospitality gifts that I use today as a pastor's wife in my queer community.

I began researching the Religious Right and their politics of hatred against people like me. To do this, I began reading the Bible while looking for some Bible scholar to help me wade through this complex book. I took note that the Bible was an engaging literary display of every genre and trope and type. It had edgy poetry, deep and complex philosophy, and compelling narrative stories. It also embodied a worldview that I hated. Sin. Repentance. Sodom and Gomorrah. Absurd.

At this time, the Promise Keepers came to town and parked their little circus at the university. In my war against stupid, I wrote an article published in the local newspaper. It was 1997.

A lot of Christians hated that article, and many wrote letters to me about how I was going to hell. One letter, from Ken Smith, was different from the rest. I liked its tone. And its author was a neighbour. I responded to this one letter, and Ken and I became friends. Real friends. Not friendship evangelism. I was not a project to Ken. I was a neighbor, and Ken taught me that Christians value neighbors.

With the letter, Ken initiated two years of bringing the church to me. Oh, I had seen my share of Bible verses on placards at gay pride marches. That Christians who mocked me at Gay Pride Day were happy that I and everyone I loved were going to hell was as clear as the sky is blue. But Ken's letter did not mock; it engaged. So when he invited me to dinner at his house to discuss these matters more fully, I accepted. My motives at the time were clear: surely this would be good for my research.

When we ate together, Ken prayed in a way that I had never heard before. His prayers were intimate. Vulnerable. He repented of his sin in front of me. He thanked God for all things. Ken's God was holy and firm, yet full of mercy. At my first meal at their home, Ken and Floy omitted two important steps in the rulebook of how Christians should deal with a heathen like me: 1) they did not share the gospel with me, and 2) they did not invite me to church. Because of these omissions to the Christian rulebook as I had come to know it, I felt that when Ken extended his hand to me in friendship, it was safe to close my hand in his.

I started meeting with Ken and Floy regularly, reading the Bible in earnest, with pen in hand and notebook in lap. I read the way a glutton devours. I became close friends with a member of the church, a man my age with my complex history of sexual sin, but who had made a profession of faith and had become a follower of this man-God Jesus. He helped me along with my Bible reading and questions. A year later, this man and I became engaged (long story here, and you will have to read *Secret Thoughts* to get a fuller one). When he dumped me, that was when I knew that I belonged to Christ alone. I will be ever grateful for this face-plant of a lesson, but also for what he modelled for me: how to read the Bible, in big chunks, reading it from Genesis to Revelation many times in one year.

I read the Bible like that the first year, arguing with its gender politics and its statements about slavery. But I kept reading it. Slowly and over time, the Bible started to take on a life and meaning that startled me. Some of my well-worn paradigms no longer stuck. As I studied the Bible, I found answers to my initial accusations.

The Bible declares itself an owner's manual of the human race. While I loathed this description, a little part of me was starting to see how Genesis 3 and Romans 1 stood out as the table of contents of what ails the world. Indeed, Romans 1 does not end by highlighting homosexuality as the worst and most extreme example of the sin of failing to give God the glory for creating us. Here is where this passage finds its crescendo:

Being filled with all unrighteousness, wickedness, greed, evil; full of envy, murder, strife, deceit, malice; they are gossips, slanderers, haters of God, insolent, arrogant, boastful, inventors of evil; disobedient to parents, without understanding, untrustworthy, unloving, unmerciful; and although they know the ordinance of God, that those who practice such things are worthy of death, they not only do the same, but also give hearty approval to those who practice them (vv. 29-32).[1]

Homosexuality, then, is not the end-point of the problem, for God or for the world. But it is presented here as one step in the journey. Homosexuality seemed then consequential, not causal. Homosexuality, from God's point of view, is an identity-rooted ethical outworking of Original Sin. Thousands of years before I was born, in the garden, when sin entered the world, Adam's fall rendered my deep and primal feelings untrustworthy and untrue. According to the Bible itself, homosexuality – and the heterosexual sexual sin that I had committed – was not the root of all sin, not even the root of my sin. Romans had already cinched it for me: sexual sin is a fruit of something larger than its own desire.

> *I prayed...that God would give me the willingness to obey before I understood.*

I had taught, studied, read, and lived a very different notion of homosexuality.

For the first time in my life, I wondered if I was wrong.

This stopped me in my tracks.

Somehow it was easier to hate the Bible when it squared off against me. When it seemed to arbitrarily single me out and oppress or marginalize me and people like me, it was

---

1   NASB 1995.

easy to dismiss. But now that it was getting under my skin it became a foe of a different and more menacing kind.

I straddled two worlds and two lives for two years. Some days, I felt like the worst of all hypocrites. And that's because I was. Other days, I felt like a true liberal, truly loving and abiding with people who were so different from me. And this was true, too.

Was I double-minded? Was I counting the costs? Yes. To both.

After years and years of this, something happened. The Bible got to be bigger inside me than I.

It overflowed into my world.

I fought against it with all my might.

I prayed...that God would give me the willingness to obey before I understood. Starting with my own sexuality was too scary, too impossible. So I started with Jesus. I prayed that God would be pleased to reveal his Son in me. I prayed that I would be a vessel of Jesus. I prayed that God would make me a godly woman – and then I laughed out loud at the insanity of this prayer. I prayed that God would give me the faith to repent of my sin at its foundation. What was the root of my sin?

How does one repent of a sin that doesn't feel like sin at all, but rather a normal not-bothering-another-soul kind of life? How had I come to this place? What was the root of the sin of sexual identity? Being a lesbian was not just a description of the kind of sex I liked to have. Being a lesbian encompassed a whole range of feelings and perceptions, character qualities, and sensibilities. And, I was a jumble of emotions, because according to the Bible, what I called community, God called idolatry.

I did not know what to do, so I prayed the way I had heard Ken pray. He often would call upon the Lord to teach him this or that. So I prayed that the Lord would help me to see my life from his point of view. It was then that I noticed it; as I looked around my house, I had dozens of PRIDE posters, T-shirts, coffee mugs. The flag

> *In the LGBT community, the opposite of pride is self-hatred. But in the Bible, the opposite of pride is faith.*

that waved in the breeze at my porch was a PRIDE flag.

Pride had become my best friend. In the LGBT world, we defined pride as a healthy self-esteem. But something started to crack a little and I dared to just ask the question: was I domesticating a tiger? Without gay pride, where would I be? Where would any of us be? In the LGBT community, the opposite of pride is self-hatred. But in the Bible, the opposite of pride is faith. Was pride keeping me from faith, or was pride keeping me from self-hatred?

That was when the question inserted itself like a foot in the door: Did pride distort self-esteem the way lust distorts love? This was the first of my many betrayals against the LGBT community: whose dictionary did I trust? The one used by the community that I helped create or the one that reflected the God who created me? As soon as the question formed itself into words, I felt convicted of the sin of pride. Pride was my downfall. I asked God for the mercy to repent of my pride at its root.

Then, one ordinary day, I came to Jesus. No altar calls in a Reformed Presbyterian Church, so no fanfare or manipulation. We were singing from Psalm 119:56: 'This is mine because forever all Thy precepts I preserve.' Two weight-bearing retaining walls collapsed in my mind. The first wall came crashing down because I had just sung condemnation

SEXUAL SIN AND IDENTITY

unto myself. This Bible was not mine. I had scorned it and cursed it and despised it.

Here was the shattering of the second wall: I had read the Bible many times through, and I saw for myself that it had a holy Author; I saw for myself that it was a canonized collection of sixty-six books with a unified biblical revelation. I heard for myself that when the words 'This is mine' came out of my mouth in congregational singing, I was attesting to this one, simple truth: that the line of communication that God ordained for his people required this wrestling with Scripture, and that I truly wanted both to hear God's voice breathed in my life, and I wanted God to hear my pleas.

The fog burned away. The whole Bible, each jot and tittle, was my open highway to a holy God.

My hands let go of the wheel of self-invention. I came to Jesus alone, open-handed, and naked. I had no dignity upon which to stand. As an advocate for peace and social justice, I thought that I was on the side of kindness, integrity, and care. It was thus a crushing revelation to discover that it was Jesus I had been persecuting the whole time – not just some historical figure named Jesus, but my Jesus, my Prophet, my Priest, my King, my Savior, my Redeemer, my Friend. That Jesus.

In this war of worldviews, Ken and Floy were there. A friend in the church, R, who had become my best champion, was there for me. The church who had been praying for me for years was there. Jesus triumphed. And I was a broken mess. I lost everything but the dog.[2]

---

2 Adapted from chapter 1, Rosaria Champagne Butterfield, *Openness Unhindered: Further Thoughts of an Unlikely Convert on Sexual Identity and Union with Christ* (Pittsburgh, Pennsylvania: Crown & Covenant Publications, 2015). Reproduced with permission.

Therefore, if anyone is in Christ, the new creation has come. The old has gone, the new is here! (2 Cor. 5:17)

❧

Do I have a sexual identity?

Most of us have probably imbibed some of the tenets of current queer theory. We are told that people with different sexual preferences, attractions or identities are 'born that way' (a change from the 1990s, when sexuality was considered a matter of choice), and that this constitutes a foundation-block of their very identity.

Dr Butterfield cautions against the use of the term 'gay Christian', because it defines a person along the lines of their sexuality as well as their 'in Christ-ness'. She admits that there are some Same-Sex Attracted (SSA) Christians who find the label 'gay Christian' helps other church members understand where their struggles lie, but she makes a strong case for discarding the term.

> Everyone loses when we define ourselves using categories that God does not.... [In Foucault's writings in the 1970s] Sexuality moved from verb (practice) to noun (people), and with this grammatical move, a new concept of humanity was born – the idea that we are oriented or framed by our sexual desires; that our differing sexual desires and different objects of desire made up separate species of people, and that self-representation and identity rooted now in sexual

---

Dr Butterfield writes her story in more detail in her first book, *Secret Thoughts of an Unlikely Convert* (Pittsburgh, Pennsylvania: Crown & Covenant Publications, 2012), which I also thoroughly recommend.

orientation, and not in the purposes of God for his image bearers. In Foucault's words, '...The sodomite had been a temporary aberration; the homosexual was a new species.'[3]

Are SSA people born that way? Is God to 'blame' for our sexual temptations? What we know is that we are, every one of us, in a battle against sin. Sam Allberry says: 'Desires for things God has forbidden are a reflection of how sin has distorted me, not how God has made me.'[4]

Does God hate gay people? Are homosexuals worse than other people?

Alongside gay marches and on rare American street corners you may have seen particularly conservative Christians holding up signs with captions such as 'God hates gays', and verses such as Leviticus 18:22, which describes homosexuality as an abomination in God's sight.

The Bible makes it very clear that God hates sin. He hates it in every manifestation, because He knows that sin is what enslaves His people. The 'freer' that society says we are to indulge our every passion, the more confused we become, like a moral Babel. Paul lists homosexuality alongside other sexual immorality, falsehood, and dishonouring parents as things that Christians should never be seen partaking in. You will know that, if you have told a lie or had a fight with a parent, you feel 'enslaved' by the secret you're keeping or the open wound of

---

3   *Openness Unhindered*, pp. 96-97.

4   Ibid., p. 134, quoting from *Is God Anti-Gay? And Other Questions about Homosexuality, the Bible and Same-Sex Attraction* (Purcellville, VA: The Good Book Company, 2013), p. 32.

your relationship. So it is with our sex lives too; living in sin – regardless of what kind – makes us feel dirty, enslaved, and far from God. Sin brings guilt, natural consequences such as disease and disunity, and ultimately spiritual and physical death. No wonder the God of freedom, restoration and life hates it!

Dr Butterfield wrote, 'I was not converted out of homosexuality, I was converted out of unbelief.'[5] What has always struck me in her story is not that a gay woman would come to Christ, but that a committed atheistic intellectual would come to Christ, with the humility of mind that that entails. There's a reason why Micah 6:8 says, 'What does the Lord require of you but...to walk humbly with your God?' Regardless of our struggles with sexual temp-

For gay Christians, Christ's command is a very literal 'Leave everything; come and follow me.' But let's not forget that it's not only a command, but also an invitation.

tation – and, as Sam Alberry writes, 'We need to be clear, not just that we are all sinners, but that we are all sexual sinners'[6] – the most important thing is to walk humbly before God, asking Him honestly and frequently to show us where we have sinned against Him and help to repent for good.

Can I change? Do I have to?

Many of us have a particular issue that defines our spiritual struggles. For some people it's anger, for some sex, for some

5   Ibid., p. 51.

6   Ibid., p. 4, quoting from *Is God Anti-Gay?*, p. 77.

fear, for some worldliness. Most of these are primarily inward wars, fighting against our own inclinations and selfishness. For gay people, living for Christ can also mean separating yourself from a partner, from friends who lead you into temptation, from a tight-knit community, from your politics. For gay Christians, Christ's command is a very literal 'Leave everything; come and follow me.' But let's not forget that it's not only a command, but also an invitation. It's an invitation we are to extend lovingly and freely in faith that He who invites will also convict of sin. One of the most beautiful verses in all Scripture is an invitation from the Bridegroom to the Bride: 'Rise up, my love, my fair one, and come away. For lo, the winter is past, the rain is over and gone.'[7] It's a coming away to a tender Father, a new community, a ready-built family. It may take some time for new Christians to cut their ties to the old and fully embrace the new. If you are struggling with SSA today, know that this verse, with all its intimacy and purity, is for you.

What you must do, however, is count the cost. Does God sometimes change sexual attraction? He can. But, like the three Israelites going into the fiery furnace, you have to approach the commitment in terms of 'but if not'. 'But if not [if God does not rescue us], let it be known to you, O king, that we do not serve your gods....'[8] If you struggle with SSA all your life, is sex itself too big a sacrifice to lay on God's altar? Be honest with yourself here, and know that you will sometimes be in

---

7   Song of Solomon 2:10-11, NKJV.

8   Daniel 3:18.

desperate need of help to keep yourself pure – not only from physical relationships, but from the temptations of solitude too. Don't be ashamed of this. God already fully sees and knows you. He doesn't judge those who come to Him for help – He helps them. 'If we stand in Christ, we are not alone,' Dr Butterfield encourages us. 'If we stand in our own self-defense, we place ourselves in exile.'[9] Walk through your temptation and your past with Christ.

Many SSA Christians who come to Christ long to change their sexual attraction, though Dr Butterfield cautions that gay conversion therapy makes the mistake of setting 'this shift into heterosexuality as its most treasured goal, and bypassing the importance of glorifying Christ in our struggle.'[10] She goes on to say: 'But I do not read sanctification in the light of a dramatic change of feelings, but rather, in the heart change that lives sacrificially for Christ in obedience to his will, in spite of feelings that run counter to God's command.'[11]

Can I bear fruit?

If you are a same-sex-attracted Christian, you can absolutely bear fruit. In fact, as a minority voice in the Christian community, you have a unique message toward Christians about their same-sex-attracted brothers and sisters, and you can be a bridge-builder with gay friends, showing them that God's hope and salvation is for them too. Living as an SSA Christian does take humility, repentance and self-denial – but

9   *Openness Unhindered*, p. 189.

10   Ibid., p. 141.

11   Ibid., p. 143.

God forgives sin;
He does not heal sin.

that should be the case for all of us redeemed sinners! Dr Butterfield writes, 'I try to live as an "out" Christian'[12] – and we all need that courage.

What does not bear fruit is compromise. Can you be in a gay relationship and still believe in Jesus for salvation? Yes – but be aware that you are holding back one area of your life as more important than Jesus, and that is a dangerous place to be:

> When we defend our right to a particular sin, when we claim it as an 'I am,' or a defining character trait, we are cherishing it, and separating ourselves from the God who promises rest for our soul through repentance and forgiveness...God forgives sin; he does not heal sin. Indeed, there is something deeply deceptive about praying that God would give me only what I need to be strong in myself. The strength that the gospel promises is the strength found only in continued dependence upon Christ.[13]...Something about seeing grace as the solution to shame didn't make sense to me. It felt to me like a step was missing. I would later learn that the missing step was repentance, and that this could be for someone a deadly step to miss.[14]

Who do I belong to?

I wonder when was the last time you included your Christianity in your identity, rather than your personality. Very often (with

---

12   Ibid., p. 33.

13   Ibid., p. 55.

14   Ibid., p. 60.

the exception of 'professional' Christians like ministers and missionaries) we are more than willing to talk about our job and place of birth and family when meeting a new person, but any mention of our beliefs is put off for weeks, until someone asks what we're doing on the weekend and we gingerly confess our plan to attend a church service – then congratulate ourselves for 'sharing our faith'! That is no doubt a careful, safe, socially correct way to admit we are Christians – though still open to scoffing from much 'cooler' atheists and agnostics – but it is not God's way.

In the Bible, there is no question of the identity of the Christian. We have died to sin, but are alive in Christ.[15] Christ presents us to the Father 'in him'.[16] We are described as members of His Body.[17] Through Communion, we become one with *His* body. What about all our other identifiers – our place in the world, in our family? 'In the resurrection they neither marry nor are given in marriage.'[18] 'My mother and brothers are those who hear the word of God and do it.'[19] 'Whoever loves [family] more than me is not worthy of me.'[20] 'There is neither Jew or Greek, there is neither slave or free, there is neither male nor female, for you are all one in Christ Jesus.'[21]

---

15   Romans 6:11.

16   2 Cor. 5:21.

17   1 Cor. 12:27, NKJV.

18   Matthew 22:30, NKJV.

19   Luke 8:21, NKJV.

20   Matthew 10:37.

21   Galatians 3:28.

None of this is to say that these things are completely irrelevant on the earth – Paul, among others, gives plenty of instructions on how to live as a family, or as a man or woman, or even how to navigate the world as a Jew or Gentile – but Jesus Himself, and the writers who followed Him, are all very clear. When you become a Christian, your primary identity is as a representative of Christ on earth, and when you die, your eyes will be so focused on Him that your primary relationship with other created beings becomes that of co-worshipper.

There is no more radical identity shift than that of non-Christian to Christian. It is as stark as moving from death to life. But it's not just a change of status before God, it's a change of relationship to God. Suddenly you are adopted! You are a daughter. You belong. You have an inheritance and a place in the royal household. At the same time (because our relationship with Him is so full and rich that no one analogy is perfect), you are the Bride of Christ. Your place is at His side, and it's an honoured and cherished place. You are embraced and adored. All the vows and promises of the Bible are yours.

Now it is Christ who defines you, and His banner over you is love. He must increase, and you must decrease.[22] That sounds sacrificial, and yet there is joy in it. Everything that you see and do and say is now through the focus of the Bible, and through the eyes of Christ, who always walks beside you. He calls this 'abiding in me', and it is a place of rest and delight and comfort and fruitfulness.

---

22   John 3:30.

*Looking to Jesus, the founder and perfecter of our faith, who
for the joy that was set before him endured the cross, despising
the shame, and is seated at the right hand of the throne of God.
(Heb. 12:2, ESV)*

What was the joy set before Him? Dear sister, you and I were.
Whose was the shame? Dear sister, yours and mine. Whose
is the victory when He sat down at God's right hand? Dear
sister, *His* – and ours. Let us fix our eyes on Him.

Questions

1. How do you describe yourself to a new acquaintance? In
   what things are you tempted to find your identity instead
   of 'in Christ'?
2. How has your life changed since you have been 'abiding in
   Christ' – or what would it look like if you 'abided' more fully?
3. Are there sinful attitudes or habits in your life of which
   you have repented but find it hard to let go of the guilt? If
   so, ask the Lord to put His 'yoke' upon you – to let Him
   bear the weight of guilt, which He has already paid for,
   and keep you close and in step with Him.

*No guilt in life, no fear in death:
This is the power of Christ in me.
From life's first cry to final breath,
Jesus commands my destiny.
No power of hell, no scheme of man
Can ever pluck me from his hand
Till he returns or calls me home
Here in the power of Christ I stand.*
—'In Christ Alone', Stuart Townend & Keith Getty

2 Difficult Marriage and Divorce

Joy Davidman

Joy Davidman is best known as the wife of C.S. Lewis – but her story started very differently. She was born in 1915, into a prosperous New York City and a family of atheist Jews. Conditioned to earn her difficult father's love as best she could, the precocious Joy declared her own atheism before she reached her teens. She kept her love for science fiction and fantasy literature secret, knowing deep down that it demonstrated a yearning for wider spiritual experiences and answers. When she was fourteen, America entered the Great Depression. Without any faith to answer her questions about poverty, injustice and suffering, Joy looked elsewhere for an ideology that made sense and offered a way to make a difference. As a young woman – now a writer – she turned to the Communist Party in America. She became the editor and famously scathing critic for their magazine, and through the Party she met fellow novelist William (Bill) Gresham. Bill proved to be an alcoholic, abusive and chronically unfaithful.

The couple had two sons in short order, but in 1946 their marriage reached a crisis point.

In Her Own Words

My husband had been overworking. One day he telephoned me from his New York office – I was at home in Westchester with the children – to tell me that he was having a nervous breakdown. He felt his mind going; he couldn't stay where he was and he couldn't bring himself to come home....Then he rang off.

There followed a day of frantic and vain telephoning. By nightfall there was nothing left to do but wait and see if he turned up, alive or dead. I put the babies to sleep and waited. For the first time in my life I felt helpless; for the first time my pride was forced to admit that I was not, after all, 'the master of my fate' and 'the captain of my soul'. All my defences – the walls of arrogance and cocksureness and self-love behind which I had hid from God – went down momentarily. And God came in.

How can one describe the direct perception of God? It is infinite, unique; there are no words, there are no comparisons. Can one scoop up the sea in a teacup? Those who have known God will understand me; the others, I find, can neither listen nor understand.

There was a Person with me in the room, directly present to my consciousness – a Person so real that all my previous life was by comparison mere shadow play. And I myself was more alive than I had ever been; it was like waking from sleep. So intense a life cannot be endured for long by flesh and blood; we must ordinarily take our life watered down, diluted as it were, by time and space and matter. My perception of God lasted perhaps half a minute.

In that time, however, many things happened. I forgave some of my enemies. I understood that God had always been there, and that, since childhood, I had devoted half my energies into the task of keeping him out. I saw myself as I really was, with dismay and repentance; and, seeing, I changed. I have been turning into a different person since that half minute, everyone tells me.

When it was over I found myself on my knees, praying. I think I must have been the world's most astonished atheist....

When my husband came home, he accepted my experience without question; he was himself on the way to something of the kind. Together, in spite of illness and anxiety, we set about remaking our minds. For obviously they needed it. If my knowledge of God was true, the thinking of my whole life had been false.[1]

Joy explored different religions, searching for the source of her experience with the divine.

...only one of them had complete understanding of the grace and repentance and charity that had come to me from God. And the Redeemer that had made himself known, whose personality I would have recognized among ten thousand – well, when I read the New Testament, I recognized him. It was Jesus.

...My present hope is twofold. I want to go deeper into the mystical knowledge of God, and I want that knowledge

---

1   All quotes in this section are from Don W. King, (Ed.) *Out of My Bone: The Letters of Joy Davidman* (Grand Rapids, MI: Eerdmans, 2009).

to govern my daily life. I had a good deal of pride and anger to overcome, and at times my progress is heartbreakingly slow – yet I think that I am going somewhere, by God's grace, according to plan. My present tasks are to look after my children and my husband and my garden and my house – and, perhaps, to serve God in books and letters as best I can. And my reward is a happiness such as I never dreamed possible. 'In His will is our peace.'

In time Bill and Joy both professed faith and held offices (elder and deaconess) in their local Presbyterian church. While Joy's spiritual life deepened and grew – through both the Bible and the works of C.S. Lewis, who became her pen-pal – Bill's did not. His interest in biblical Christianity waned in favour of Scientology's Dianetics as well as other spiritualist fads. After ten years of marriage, Joy left her two sons with Bill, with her cousin Renée and her two children looking after them, and spent several months in England, where she met Lewis. While she was away, Bill wrote her a long, callous, self-centred letter asking for a divorce in order to marry Renée. He offered Dianetics as the best way for the three of them to unload their negative feelings and live near each other to raise the children. While Joy was initially shocked by Bill's request for a divorce, she found that the total breakdown of the marriage gave her the freedom to both see and call out Bill for the kind of husband he had been, and when he tried to bully and threaten her into taking him back, she could not bear the thought of it.

[To Chad Walsh, a Christian friend and writer] I don't know how you feel about divorce. I always took it that divorce was only the last possible resort, and felt I ought to put up with anything I could bear for the children's sake. And I hoped that Bill's adulteries, irresponsibilities, etc. would end if he ever recovered from his various neuroses; also that his becoming a Christian would make a difference. Unfortunately I've been disappointed on both counts. Bill gave up being a Christian as soon as he found out it meant living by a moral code and admitting and repenting one's sins.

...I never felt I could talk to anybody about my married life, in the past. But when this new situation developed I asked Lewis for advice and told him a good deal of the story – an expurgated version, at that. Some of it I simply can't put into words. Anyhow Lewis strongly advised me to divorce Bill; and has repeated it even more strongly since I've been home – Bill greeted me by knocking me about a bit, and I wrote Lewis about that. So now I'm rid of the feeling that it's my duty to go on!

She even shared her experiences with her husband's mistress when she had herself been let down by Bill.

[To Renée] One of the things about being the victim of such a man is the self-contempt it brings – the woman despises herself for being a fool and a sucker....I am a fairly bright girl, and yet I was so much under Bill's influence that I had to run away from him physically and consult one of the clearest thinkers of our time for help, before I could see clearly what he was!...[Bill] went on to say that a neurotic's promises oughtn't to be considered binding and that a 'rapidly changing personality' like his couldn't be held to any promise. In short, he's entitled to be fickly because he's fickle.

Joy also took her children's relationship with their father into account when thinking about the family's future.

> [to Chad Walsh]...All the same, I've been thinking and praying hard since I saw you, trying to be sure that I am doing the right thing. Jack [Lewis] wrote me a few days ago, saying what I thought myself; that I must disregard my own feelings and base my decision on what is best for the boys. The boys, Davy particularly, beg me not to take Bill back – they say he makes them nervous and jumpy, and Lord knows I've seen it happen! Worse yet, I think, is what they learn from him – I've known both of them to try tantrums just like his on me.

Bill and Joy divorced in 1952 and Joy took the boys to live in England. Bill paid a fraction of the child support ordered by the court, and Joy tried to sell what writing she could, including a study of the Ten Commandments, *Smoke on the Mountain*. Joy and Lewis' relationship deepened, and they married civilly in 1956 to solve a visa problem. A year later, with Joy suffering from cancer, they had a bedside wedding performed by an Anglican priest. Her prognosis was deeply uncertain.

> [to Chad Walsh]...the physical agony was combined with a strange spiritual ecstasy; I think I know now how martyrs felt. All this has strengthened my faith and brought me very close to God – as if at last I knew all the answers.

Joy entered a stunning remission that gave her three happy years, in which she and Jack travelled together, and she helped him with some of his best-known works. Deeply in love, Jack was Joy's mainstay in painful periods of bad health and further cancer scares. When Joy finally died of her illness in 1960, Lewis wrote *A Grief Observed* in her memory.

Trust in him at all times, you people; pour out your hearts to him, for God is our refuge. (Ps. 62:8)

⁓

Can you overcome?

Some of you reading this chapter know all too well the agony of emotional and physical abuse, addiction or unfaithfulness in your marriage. You're wondering how you'll survive, or how you'll ever feel yourself again. You're wondering how God could let you get into this terrible place. But you can't blame God completely, because you also blame yourself. You question your choices and reactions and even your standing before God. Even if you have never been married, perhaps you know the sensation of your life going a way you never pictured it – never wanted it to. You may have relationships with friends, colleagues or family members that feel toxic or even abusive.

Others of you have had a marriage fail long ago, perhaps even before your conversion, and feel uneasy about the decisions you made. There are regrets and consequences for your choices, and the past seems to follow you. Do you really have a place among the 'good' people at church?

Some of you have gone through a bad patch in your marriage which has shaken your view of your spouse and your faith too. Perhaps you are there now: you knew all marriages had rough spots, but you're certain it isn't meant to be this hard. You're wondering if there's a way for your marriage to experience joy again, or perhaps longing for a way out but unsure of the biblical mandate to leave.

Or you may be one of the many Christian couples that has a loving, faithful, supportive marriage, but you are aware of the cracks that show up in any union between two sinners. Irritations surface; resentments over housework and money simmer; two sex drives move at different speeds; one spouse tends to compromise more on big decisions. You know those are normal issues, but it's hard to remember sometimes that you're on the same team.

There are a number of different points of view on the biblical doctrine of divorce, though perhaps the more controversial subject is remarriage. It's not the purpose of this book to explore these issues, and I'd encourage you to do some research and speak to your minister or elder if you need biblical counsel on these topics. Our question is simply: can you still be fruitful in your Christian life? Can you overcome?

For struggling wives

Let's look first at what *overcoming* looks like in a difficult marriage, whether it's an abusive situation or simply a loveless or tense relationship.

First, where there is physical danger, any church should advise the woman to at least separate from her husband. A situation with physical violence is bad for the wife, bad for the children, and even bad for the husband: by beating or molesting his wife he is committing criminal acts which are hardening his heart, and it is better for him to be denied that opportunity. Guilt should not keep a woman captive in a physically threatening situation. Women who have been abused are often subject to threats or manipulation, and need courage and strength from Christ, and support from the church, to make that step.

Where safety is not an issue but the marriage itself is deeply broken, *The Emotionally Destructive Marriage* by Leslie Vernick suggests that a wife should decide 'to stay well or to leave well'.[2] I would suggest that staying 'well' in a struggling marriage means full commitment to the instruction of 1 Peter 3:1 (ESV): 'Likewise, wives, be subject to your own husbands, so that even if some do not obey the word, they may be won without a word by the conduct of their wives...'

This is deeply unpalatable advice – and every bit as revolutionary in the twenty-first century as it was in the first. It essentially tells wives to treat unbelieving husbands with all the respect they would give to a husband who properly fulfils the role of spiritual headship in the home. It calls for a level of restraint, servanthood, and proactive kindness that will feel actually unjust if you don't keep in mind the ultimate aim of winning your husband for Christ. It requires that a wife who longs for her husband's love, and feels the sting of his neglect, anger or scorn deeply day after day, commit to looking for her fulfilment in Christ instead, taking her comfort from Him. It means a life of fasting and prayer, of speaking to a husband about Jesus lovingly without guilt-tripping him, of refusing to enable serious sin while resisting the temptation to nag your spouse about every shortcoming!

---

2   Vernick, Leslie. *The Emotionally Destructive Marriage: How to Find Your Voice and Reclaim Your Hope* (Waterbrook/Multnomah, 2013).

I believe this is (to an extent) good advice for other damaging relationships in our lives too. Where there is a truly toxic presence in your life, it is wise to avoid that person – but, where you do encounter them, there may be blessing and restoration if you can show them the dignity, kindness and wisdom of Christ, so that they too may be won without a word.

Finally, it's hard but vital to take a look at our own hearts. All difficult marriages are between two sinners, and no sinner goes through an intimate relationship without contributing her own faults and mistakes. These can become systemic without us even realising it, and taking a hard honest look at our own hearts is the first step in healing any struggling marriage. While Bill Gresham was undoubtedly a terrible husband, Joy also made fatal errors in her first marriage; she was probably in an emotional affair with C.S. Lewis (albeit one-sided) even before visiting England. God knows our hearts, and our spouse's shortcomings never excuse our own. At the same time, we can cry out to our Father when we feel brokenness in our relationships, and know that He hears us. We can repent of our own sins and know that we are forgiven, and seek help and strength when we find ourselves slipping toward them again.

Is it possible to have peace in the Lord while still living in a tense and loveless home? **Yes.** We are commanded to give thanks in all circumstances, and it is our thankful hearts that are our greatest witness to Christ in us. If we can live with serenity and integrity, that will always be attractive to those around us. To do so takes commitment to spiritual discipline: lifting your eyes to Christ must become habitual, not occasional, to achieve joy in a barren land.

For remarriage

Matthew 5:32 states, 'whoever marries a divorced woman commits adultery'. If you're a Christian woman reading this chapter, you've probably already heard that verse – maybe more times than you care to remember. The context is that Jesus is telling the Pharisees their moral code is not enough; God demands to go beyond the letter of the law and rule even their thoughts and intentions. Some churches interpret the Bible to mean that a second marriage is valid if the first was broken by abuse or adultery; others (like the Church of England in Joy's time) take a more conservative view. So, what if you are divorced and remarried, or married to a divorcé? Can you overcome that start to your marriage? **Yes.**

Let's look at the story of David and Bathsheba. Their adultery had dire consequences for Bathsheba's first husband, for their child, for David's wider family, for his reign and for all of Israel. Yet God blessed their marriage with the birth of Solomon, a king famous for his wisdom and the grandeur of his rule. God is in the business of healing relationships and families and turning what started as a bad situation into one that brings glory to Him.

You may consider your remarriage a moral dilemma, or you may see it as nothing but a gift from God. Either way, you are called to minister to your husband now as your one and only! You are in a marriage and your role is to be faithful, loving, fully committed, and point him and others to Christ. Joy

Davidman found her greatest fulfilment and widest witness as the wife of C.S. Lewis. Regardless of the ways she contributed to the end of her first marriage, God gave her joy and blessing through her second. Wherever you are now, and whomever you're married to, your chief role in life is to serve and glorify God.

Coping with kids

If you are a single parent after divorce, or your husband has a negative or neglectful impact on your children, then your two chief concerns are your children's safety and spiritual upbringing. If the situation at home has become physically threatening or you fear your husband may in any way abuse the children, you should get them out of that situation at once. If they are observing other negative behaviours from him, then don't make excuses for your husband (lest the children think his actions are acceptable), but speak to them honestly without adding to the blame yourself. It does not help for you to complain, offload on them, or over-explain your spouse's behaviour.

In looking after the children's spiritual wellbeing, simple may be best: Bible stories at bedtime, prayers at meals or on the way to school, singing psalms or hymns around the house. It's vital that you not allow Satan's twin lies of guilt and shame to keep you from public worship with your kids. Church is where you receive balm for your soul, support when it's needed, examples of godly men for your sons to emulate and a non-toxic family atmosphere.

Most important of all is your personal lifestyle of consistency, service and love for Christ. Share your testimony and spiritual growth with your children. Ask their forgiveness if you forget a promise or lose your temper. Hold them to account in living according to God's way. And remind them that Jesus is always there for them in their own doubt and confusion. While it's easy for a negative home atmosphere to affect your own moods and reactions, pray for yourself Paul's prayer of being 'rooted and grounded in love' (Eph. 3:17). If you are rooted and grounded in your worth and standing before Christ, you will bear the fruit of gentleness and godliness before your whole family. Not dissimilarly to Rosaria Butterfield's change of identity, you must remember that your identity is who CHRIST says you are, not who your husband or children want you to be.

> *If we can catch even a glimpse of what Christ wants to accomplish through our hardest uphill struggles, it becomes easier to say 'I can walk with you a little further, now that I see where you are leading.'*

One of the better-known examples of a bad Christian marriage was that of Samuel and Susanna Wesley, the parents of John and Charles. Samuel Wesley insisted on complete authoritarianism within his home. His view of Scripture was that of a husband's complete power. Accordingly, he took issue with his wife's difference of political opinion, and used it as an excuse to abandon the family for months. Eventually he returned when a house fire made it necessary, but he apparently never repented. Susanna was deeply wounded and grieved by her husband's behaviour – and this was not the only example of his abuse of power – but she founded her sense of reality and worth in the Lord, and poured her energies into her children's spiritual growth. She also consistently showed her husband respect even when she was aware he was in grievous error, and prayed for him instead of allowing bitterness to flourish.[3]

Repentance and suffering: hard-won freedom

The fact is that trial and tragedy come to all people, whether they are Christians or not. Christ's love and help are available to all – but not everyone allows Him to work through the worst of times. And not everyone makes those times fruitful; some become resentful or despairing. If we can catch even a glimpse of what Christ wants to accomplish through our hardest uphill struggles, it becomes easier to say 'I can walk with you a little further, now that I see where you are leading.' I would encourage you, if you feel you are battling through storm and wind, to look intently for where Christ might be working in your character or in those around you as you respond to His discipline. Don't let your suffering be of no account. Instead be moulded and refined: actively look for it. This is where you find freedom within your hard present, and freedom from your past.

---

3   Arthur Dallimore's *Susanna Wesley: The Mother of John and Charles Wesley* (Ada, MI: Baker Publishing, 1993) contains an entire chapter on this incident, including several letters Susanna wrote to spiritual shepherds who were able to support her emotionally and practically. The chapter is tough reading, but instructive for those in similar situations.

Looking at Joy Davidman's story, it's interesting to trace the line of God's work in her life through her bad experiences. It was through a crisis point in her marriage that Jesus revealed

every element of her life which experienced death led to her greater growth and fruitfulness

Himself to her, as her desperation threw her on His mercy. It was while Bill fluttered from one spiritual fad to another, and back to a sinful lifestyle, that Joy discovered her roots growing deeper into Christianity and wrote her own story of faith. It was through cancer that Joy's second marriage truly began, and it was through her death that C.S. Lewis wrote one of the world's best books on grieving, which has helped millions in their bereavement. Joy was not always an easy woman to love, but her character was like the seed that must die in order to create new life – every element of her life which experienced death led to her greater growth and fruitfulness. She was not perfect, but she was willing to subject her life to her Lord and see Him change her.

Having an imperfect marriage is a blessing in one way: it shows you with perfect clarity that your primary relationship is never with a spouse (even in a good marriage!), but always with Christ. As Christians we are ultimately His Bride, and

If Christ is on the throne, your spouse is not on it

He is the one Bridegroom who is always consistent, always faithful, always attentive, always kind. He is the reason you need not fear rejection, you need not fear your spouse, and you need not fear the future. If Christ is on the throne, your spouse is not on it; your children are not on it; and your emotions are not on it. Your heart is safe in Him.

Can I bear fruit?

Is it possible to be fruitful for God's kingdom after a divorce or remarriage? *Yes.* The choices we made in our past may have consequences and regrets, but when we have repented and committed them to the Lord, they should no longer rule or define us. God uses people who have been discouraged, who have been broken, who have felt worthless,

> *Christ came not to judge those who believe in Him, but to give us new life. That new life is not worn-out, damaged, soiled or second-best.*

even who have brought calamity on themselves. He uses them mightily, in fact – to show His grace, His renewal, His faithfulness. He restores the years the locusts have eaten.[4] He puts a new song in our mouth, a song of praise to our God.[5]

Divorce is not something God takes lightly, and therefore it must not be something that Christians take lightly. Marriage is intended to be for life. Sometimes that is not within our control, particularly if the husband leaves or becomes violent. But Christ came not to judge those who believe in Him, but to give us new life. That new life is not worn-out, damaged, soiled or second-best. That life is beautiful, glorious, and powerful!

4   Joel 2:25.

5   Psalm 40:3.

Hebrews 10:14 says, 'For by a single offering he has perfected for all time those who are being sanctified.' There are two bits of good news here. The first is that you are *perfect forever!* Can you comprehend those words? Meditate on them, internalise them, memorize them! The other is that we are *being made holy.* Even though we are legally perfect before Him, we are still growing and learning. Part of our growth in holiness is to stop being fixated on what has happened in the past, but to look for where we can serve Him now. We have *His* perfection, and therefore we are both worthy and called to serve His kingdom.

Isaiah 26:3 says, 'You keep him in perfect peace whose mind is stayed on you, because he trusts in you.' Whether in a good or bad marriage, single or divorced, remarried or widowed, we are all the perfect Bride of Christ, and there is no spot in us. We are cherished, we are seen with delight, and we are being made perfect. The scars of sin and hurt remain on our hearts in this life, but a day is coming when all things are being made new.

Questions

1. In what way does my life not conform to my expectations of it? What decisions do I regret or feel ashamed of?
2. Are there relationships where I need to 'stay well or leave well'? What do those options look like with a spouse, family member, friend or colleague who has hurt me?
3. What hard or sad places in my life can God use to make me more fruitful and in line with His character?

Be still, my soul: the Lord is on your side;
Bear patiently the cross of grief or pain;
Leave to your God to order and provide;
In ev'ry change he faithful will remain.
Be still, my soul: your best, your heav'nly Friend
Through thorny ways leads to a joyful end.
—Kathrina von Schlegel

3 Bereavement

Elisabeth Elliot

Elisabeth had always had a true love. Her life had been dedicated to Jesus Christ since early childhood; how could she resist, when she had seen her missionary parents' and her siblings' love for Him? By the time she went to university, Elisabeth knew she wanted to translate the Bible into a new language, and so she studied Classics in order to translate from the original Greek.

It was in university that she met Jim. He was intense, certain, vibrant; Elisabeth was reserved and overly thoughtful. Despite their different personalities and Jim's conviction that the Lord meant him to stay single, he soon realised that this tall, pretty, dignified woman was to be his helpmeet in his missionary work. Much of their courtship was carried out by letters – arguments and all! – and they took their time in setting out their future. Their work for God must always come first, and further training and travel had to take priority. Yet, through it all, their love remained, and deepened. It was a gift from God, and their relationship was truly a 'cord of three strands'.

In 1953, Elisabeth and Jim arrived separately in Ecuador, and were married soon after in the capital city of Quito. It was quite a honeymoon, busily learning Spanish as well as a tribal language, scoping out the base where they would minister, adapting to a new climate and diet, and meeting fellow missionaries who were in different stages of their own work. The Elliots ended up stationed near the east coast of Ecuador, ministering to a remote tribe, but soon their awareness grew of a people completely unreached. The Aucas[1] were known to be hostile to Westerners; still, Jim and Elisabeth grew in their conviction that Christ must mean to bring some of these people into His Kingdom of all nations and tongues.

Over the course of many months, several other missionaries in the region shared in the Elliots' passion for the Aucas. Contact was made possible thanks to MAF pilot Nate Saint, and the missionaries made many low flights over an Auca village, dropping gifts and calling out winsome messages in their few words of the tribal language, as they made preparations to establish a base near the village. Meanwhile, Elisabeth was entering a new sphere of life – she had a baby daughter, Valerie. Despite these fresh demands, she was intimately involved in the missionaries' planning as well as running the Elliots' own missionary base whenever Jim was

---

1   Now known as the Waodani or Huaorani people. Wheaton College will also be replacing a plaque honouring alumnus Jim Elliot in which the Waodani are referred to as 'savage'. I have maintained the usage of Auca here because that it the term used in Elisabeth's writings.

away on his forays. In January 1956, Jim and Nate, along with three other missionaries, flew to 'Palm Beach', a remote jungle riverside, to set up their Auca base.

On 8 January, Nate Saint missed his scheduled radio check-in with his wife. She didn't want to panic the other missionaries' families, and so it wasn't until the next morning that they learned something had gone awry with the mission. Remembering that moment, Elisabeth wrote, 'A verse God had impressed on my mind when I first arrived in Ecuador came back suddenly and sharply: "When thou passest through the waters, I will be with thee, and through the rivers, they shall not overflow thee…"'[2]

In the days to come a substantial rescue party was sent up to the Aucas' territory, where all five missionaries were confirmed dead, killed by the tribesmen they had gone to win for Christ. The wives gathered together to share agonising grief and a strength that could only come from the Almighty.

> In the kitchen we sat quietly as the reports were finished, fingering the watches and wedding rings that had been brought back, trying for the hundredth time to picture the scene. Which of the men watched the others fall? Which of them had time to think of his wife and children? Had one been covering the others in the tree house, and come down in an attempt to save them? Had they suffered long? The answers to these questions remained a mystery. This much we knew: 'Whosoever shall lose his life for my sake and the gospel's, the same shall save it.'[3] There was no question as to

2   Isaiah 43:2, KJV.
3   Matthew 16:25, KJV.

the present state of our loved ones. They were 'with Christ'.
...The quiet trust of the mothers helped the children to know
that this was not a tragedy. This was what God had planned.[4]

Elisabeth Elliot and Rachel Saint, the sister of pilot Nate,
were later involved in fulfilling Jim and Nate's dream – they
returned to the Aucas and saw villagers won for Christ. The
story of the 'five martyrs' has inspired millions of Christians
since. Elisabeth Elliot's experience of suffering, however, had
not ended. She lost a second husband to cancer, and the last
ten years of her life were marred by dementia. Her writings
and recordings have not only given a powerful account of
the Auca mission, but have encouraged and nurtured many
Christians in their experience of suffering.

He heals the brokenhearted and binds up their wounds.
(Ps. 147:3)

⟨≈≈⟩

Beautifying the Church

One of the verses surely most appropriate to a time of deep
grief is God's promise to give us 'beauty for ashes, the oil of
joy for mourning'.[5] It feels unfathomable, when in the depths,
that this exchange is possible: yet God proves Himself, over

---

4   All quotes are from *Through Gates of Splendour,* Elisabeth Elliot,
     (Milton Keynes, UK: Authentic Media edition 2005, first printed
     1956). This quote is from chapter 19, 'Yet Have We Not Forgotten
     Thee'.

5   Isaiah 61:3, KJV.

and over again, to be beautiful through loss, the one light in pitch darkness.

Although we had only met once in person, MC and I were firm Facebook friends. An expatriate myself, I lived in her home country of Scotland, while MC had moved to Peru to be with her husband, Erick. Our similar sense of humour, spiritual experience, and shared homesickness created a bond out of a social media relationship.

Albeit MC's past was in Scotland, her future was planted firmly in Peru. She and Erick had two little girls, and by the time they went to school, MC was taking up teaching again and soon started an additional qualification in primary education. She stretched herself thin, looking after the girls and often working late into the night on lesson plans and her thesis, but Erick was ever encouraging and supportive.

When MC finally got the chance to come home for a visit, after more than two years away from Scotland, I rejoiced with her; I knew how deeply her heart ached to come back. I looked forward to seeing her at church and finally getting to spend some time getting to know her in person.

And then, in the middle of a very joyful time in Scotland, MC's devoted and winsome husband suddenly collapsed late one night and passed away. His death is thought to be cardiac-related. MC was with him at the time.

In the weeks that followed, I observed a Church in mourning – not a single congregation, but a whole national denomination, grieving with a young woman who held no office, no particular position within its structure. They simply coalesced around a widow and her two little children:

praying passionately for them, weeping with them, donating many thousands of pounds as a support fund. In the midst of harrowing loss, the outpoured grief of the Church became something beautiful to behold. I was proud to be part of a community that was really, demonstrably bearing a young woman's burden in a way that would simply not have happened if she hadn't belonged to the Body of Christ.

There are times, even more remarkably, when the Church as a whole – missionally, culturally, and viscerally – is enriched by the death of one of its own members. This has been seen many times throughout church history, when martyrhood became the catalyst for greater change, greater sacrifice, greater understanding within the Church. Elisabeth Elliot commemorated the very beginnings of her husband's legacy:

> To the world at large this was a sad waste of five young lives. But God has His plan and purpose in all things. There were those whose lives were changed by what happened on Palm Beach. In Brazil, a group of Indians at a mission station deep in the Mato Grosso, upon hearing the news, dropped to their knees and cried out to God for forgiveness for their own lack of concern for fellow Indians who did not know of Jesus Christ. From Rome, an American official wrote to one of the widows: 'I knew your husband. He was to me the ideal of what a Christian should be.' An Air Force Major stationed in England, with many hours of jet flying, immediately began making plans to join the Missionary Aviation Fellowship. A missionary in Africa wrote: 'Our work will never be the same. We knew two of the men. Their lives have left their mark on ours.'

Off the coast of Italy, an American naval officer was involved in an accident at sea. As he floated alone on a raft, he recalled Jim Elliot's words (which he had read in a news report): 'When it comes time to die, make sure that all you have to do is die.' He prayed that he might be saved, knowing that he had more to do than die. He was not ready. God answered his prayer, and he was rescued. In Des Moines, Iowa, an eighteen-year-old boy prayed for a week in his room, then announced to his parents: 'I'm turning my life over completely to the Lord. I want to try to take the place of one of those five.'

Letters poured in to the five widows – from a college in Japan, 'We are praying for you'; from a group of Eskimo children in a Sunday School in Alaska; from a Chinese church in Houston; from a missionary on the Nile River who had picked up Time magazine and seen a photograph of her friend, Ed McCully.

Only eternity will measure the number of prayers which ascended for the widows, their children, and the work in which the five men had been engaged. The prayers of the widows themselves are for the Aucas. We look forward to the day when these savages will join us in Christian praise.[6]

God uses men and women after His own heart to beautify the Church, and through the Church, the whole world. He uses His people during their lives, and He even uses them in death.

---

6   *Through Gates of Splendour,* chapter 19, 'Yet Have We Not Forgotten Thee'.

Beautifying Scripture

It's a strange heading, I know, because Scripture is inherently beautiful. Yet great sadness has a way of bringing the beauty of the Bible to us afresh. Many of you will know the experience of reading a familiar verse in a time of distress, and finding that it feels 'alive' to you for the first time.

This is especially notable in Elisabeth Elliot's experience and those of the other widows who suffered alongside her. Barbara Youderian, widow of the martyr Roger, wrote in her diary:

> God gave me this verse two days ago, Psalm 48:14, 'For this God is our God for ever and ever; He will be our Guide even unto death.' As I came face to face with the news of Roj's death, my heart was filled with praise he was worthy of his home-going.

Elisabeth wrote:

> And, once more, ancient words from the Book of Books came to mind: 'All this has come upon us, yet have we not forgotten thee...Our heart is not turned back, neither have our steps declined from Thy way, though Thou hast sore broken us in the place of dragons, and covered us with the shadow of death.'[7]

There was no time-gap between the blow of Jim's death and the sense of Christ walking alongside her, for He had been there all along

---

7   *Through Gates of Splendour,* chapter 18, 'Silence'. The widows quote the KJV Bible – not only had the NIV not been written yet, but Elisabeth Elliot would be involved in writing it!

Sometimes the only help that can come to us in times of grief is the comfort, the encouragement, and the promises of God, spoken in God's own voice, or even just the truth that He is who He is. It is the only thing that brings real balm in the immediacy of loss and day-by-day strength in mourning. In seeing Elisabeth Elliot's description of applying particular verses to her loss – almost before she even knew it had happened – the striking thing is that she knew the Scriptures so well that they were already written on her heart. There was no time-gap between the blow of Jim's death and the sense of Christ walking alongside her, for He had been there all along as she walked in step with Him, and His words were a well that she drew upon constantly.

Prepare your heart in readiness for your own times of suffering by dwelling on the Lord's suffering. The armour of God is always sound, but it is of most immediate use when it has been properly fitted and tried out in small skirmishes; then we find it fits like a second skin when we really need the defense. This is of particular benefit to those of us who are not (yet) widows: this is the time to prepare, for as MC's story reminds us, we never know when we may need to draw on those spiritual reserves.

Beautifying the Widow

Both Christians and the outside world often carry the impression that great suffering drives us further from Christ, but not all widows have found that to be the case. Catriona Murray, a college lecturer who had long been attending her local church, described to me her experience of professing faith eleven months after her husband Donnie's death:

> I believe I'd been converted years before but had my long-absent assurance when I turned instinctively to Christ and He caught me in His arms.
>
> It was when we were told Donnie would die. Instead of the bleak devastation that I expected, I can only describe it as me turning to the Lord as a hurt child turns to a parent: so I knew that I knew Him as a Father. And because I felt – palpably felt – His surrounding love and peace during the seven days I spent in the hospice with Donnie, I knew my faith in Him was justified. That is, I knew it was real and not just a nice comfort blanket. His love that I was so aware of persuaded me that He doesn't arbitrarily hurt us; that hard providence is to a greater purpose. And, like Melanie Wilkes says to Scarlett in *Gone With the Wind*, I often say to the Lord, 'it's not likely I'd question any device of yours' – because I know Him to be thoroughly good and merciful and just.

Catriona found that all she had learned about Christ as head-knowledge during her years in the pew became her heart's reality through her experience of pain and loss. The death of her husband did not point the finger at a chaotic, unfeeling or cruel God who was indifferent to her pain; just the opposite. It pointed her *to* the God who had taken loss upon Himself, had experienced cruelty, and who held both the cosmos and her heart within His hand. As so often happens in life, He had subjected her to pain in love: a pain that would only draw her nearer to Himself, a pain that He alone was able to calm. Catriona is now a Christian columnist and blogger,[8] a faithful servant of her church, and is a local government representative. Very often, when she faces opposition in her role, she reminds herself that all of her approval, all of her needs, all of her desire, is met in Christ. These are riches that she found through widowhood.

Christian blogger Kaylene Yoder writes:

> Tears are symbolic of cleansing, releasing and healing. Psalm 56:8 speaks of the Lord holding our tears in a wineskin or bottle. I find it hard to believe that he keeps those bottles of tears on a shelf somewhere like a trophy. Rather, I believe he uses them to water new growth in us.[9]

Are you a widow? Your life of growth in Christ and fruit in Christ is not over. Let the Lord do His good work in you, using your hardship to refine you, draw you closer to Himself, and bless the work of His Kingdom. God will strengthen you in time, and use your strength to build up others. In Isaiah 61:3 here is the full, glorious picture of how the Redeemer transforms and uses our sadness:

> *[He will] provide for those who grieve in Zion—*
> *to bestow on them a crown of beauty*
> *   instead of ashes,*
> *the oil of joy*
> *   instead of mourning,*

---

8   Catriona's powerful and winsome blog can be found at posttenebraslux.co.uk

9   'Trading Trouble for Pearls,' email blog, 28/4/20. Kaylene has a wealth of prayer and devotional resources at kayleneyoder.com

and a garment of praise
*   instead of a spirit of despair.*
They will be called oaks of righteousness,
*   a planting of the Lord*
*   for the display of his splendour.*

Allow the Lord to plant you and water you, knowing that His will is to keep growing you, and through that growth, to show off His splendour!

Beautifying the Beloved

We've spoken about the effect that the death of a believer can have in beautifying the Church, Scripture and the widow. One of the most comforting verses of Scripture for a widow might be 'Precious in the sight of the Lord is the death of his saints.'[10] Why? Because that death is precious to her too. The last days and words of her beloved will remain with her as long as she lives. It is a mark of the Lord's tenderness that this moment is precious to Him too.

Very often the first question a believer will ask a bereaved fellow Christian is *'Was he a Christian?'* If the answer is yes, this is frequently followed up by the reminder that 'we do not mourn as those that have no hope' – yet we must be careful not to imply that to mean 'we do not mourn'! If even Christ wept before the grave of His friend, we should not expect His followers to be stoics who are so heavenly-minded they are numb to earthly pain.   There are some who question whether we will know one another in Heaven. But in 1 Thessalonians

---

10   Psalm 116:15, ESV.

4:13-18, this is *why* we are encouraged not to mourn as others who have no hope: *because* we will be together with the Lord. It's true that there is 'no marriage in the resurrection [in heaven]', but this signifies that our relationships will not be aimed primarily at one another: instead we will be side by side, gazing upon our risen Lord and joining in His worship. Since the purpose of this passage is to give us the comfort of reunion, we should enter fully into that comfort. But sometimes we need time to process the loss before even looking ahead to the reunion. MC said: 'One of the things I am most thankful for, looking back on the darkest days, was that people did NOT jump to the positives of our hope in Christ, or the Christian clichés. They conveyed their deep sorrow with and for me, and joined me in my "time to weep"'.

What if you ask a widow if her husband was a Christian, and she says, 'No, he didn't place his faith in Jesus'? Is there any comfort in the Bible for her?

I'm going to say this flat out: the Bible gives us no hope of reunion with those who die outside of Christ. Ultimately it is Him, and not us, who judges whether a person truly believed the Lord for salvation, but if we know that someone died at enmity with God, it is biblically unfounded to think of them 'in a better place' or 'watching over us' or 'no longer suffering'. This is a deeply painful and troubling truth.

Many Christian wives witness to their husbands both with their lives and their words for many years, only to see them die still in unbelief. Remember that, while loving and consistent witness is the wife's duty, the opening of a man's heart and eyes are in God's hand alone. Only He saves. But if her husband has refused to soften His heart to God's voice, then the separation is final. The widow is left to the comfort of her memories, her family and friends, and the balm of time. And that's not enough, is it?

pour the most precious, hardest-won thing you have, your grief, out before him like Mary pouring her fragrance

But there are also the promises. The promise of beauty for ashes, yes, but also the promise of one who wipes away every tear. The widow's solace can no longer be found in her beloved. It can only be in her Redeemer. Let's look at the verses preceding the passage we just looked at, Isaiah 61:1-2 (ESV):

> *The Spirit of the Lord God is upon me,*
>   *because the Lord has anointed me*
>   *to bring good news to the poor;*
> *He has sent me to bind up the brokenhearted,*
>   *to proclaim liberty to the captives*
>   *and the opening of the prison to those who are bound...*

God sent His Son into a broken world to bandage up broken people. Allow Him to do this. Pour your tears into His bottle; pour the most precious, hardest-won thing you have, your grief, out before Him like Mary pouring her fragrance. Entrust it to Him; give Him your captivity to loneliness, your darkness of despair. He will never tire of taking it from you, no matter how often you need to run to Him.

Elisabeth Elliot said, 'People sometimes ask me, "How did you get rid of your feelings?" I tell them I didn't get rid of them. I offer them to God, and I have to offer them again, and again, and again.'[11]

Can I bear fruit?

What is the culmination of beautifying the Church, the Scripture, the widow, and the Beloved? It is the beautifying of Him who holds all of these fast in His hand. As with Scripture, it is impossible to give to Christ more beauty than He already inherently has. But we can *ascribe* more beauty to Him. Revelation describes the 'four living creatures' and the twenty-four elders falling down before his throne: 'Worthy is the Lamb who was slain, to receive power and wealth and wisdom and might and honor and glory and blessing!'[12] Did they say this because they were able, themselves, to give Him wealth and glory? Or because they thought He did not have enough of these things? No, they said it out of the overflow of their hearts, because they could finally see with unfettered eyes how worthy He was of all things, of ultimate and unyielding recognition of His goodness and glory.

Where do we find the beauty of the Lord when our eyes are still blinded by tears?

Bereavement is one of the many circumstances the Lord uses to unfetter our vision. We beautify the Lord to ourselves, and to others, when we recognise His beauty in the midst of our ashes. When we recognise His ability to transform us,

---

11 Interview for Ligonier Ministries, 'There's No Coming to Life Without Pain', Tabletalk Magazine, 1 February 1989.

12 Revelation 5:12, ESV.

and our witness, and our world, through the worst of human pain. When, instead of blaming Him for the fallen world which causes cancer and viruses and heart disease and terrible accidents and human malice, we run to Him as the Redeemer and the Keeper of Promises.

MC testifies that her experience of great suffering has brought her into the suffering of the Saviour:

> Jesus suffered the worst kind of death, and the Father allowed that suffering for His deep love of us. I have found in the darkest despair, in the 'Why would God allow me to feel this way?', I was brought to remember the cross, Jesus sweating drops of blood, suffering slowly and dying. The Father knows, Jesus knows; God is not far from us in our despair or our darkness. God holds us when we're broken. He *knows*.

Where do we find the beauty of the Lord when our eyes are still blinded by tears?

We find it when we 'come away' with Him like the Bride in the Song of Solomon.

We find it with the 'ready writer' of Psalm 45, when we inhale the scent of our beloved.

We find it in the tears of the Creator God who cried before His friend's grave.

We find it in the Morning Star, in the Resurrection and the Life, in the one who holds the keys of death and Hades in His hand, in the tenderly spoken name of the woman who came to weep at His tomb.

Listen to Him speak your name.

Questions

1. Where is there grief or loneliness in your life? Have you invited the Lord into that pain, and how have you found His comfort in it?

2. In what way can the difficult circumstances in your life reveal more beauty in Christ, His Word, yourself as a Christian, or the Church?

3. Does the reality of heaven and hell after death motivate you to share Jesus' offer of salvation with others? If not, what is stopping you?

Because he lives, I can face tomorrow;
Because he lives, all fear is gone;
Because I know he holds the future,
And life is worth the living
Just because he lives.
—Bill Gaither

4 Singleness

Betsie & Corrie ten Boom

Betsie and Corrie ten Boom were well known for their courage, love for the peoples persecuted by the Nazis in World War Two, and stalwart proclamation of God's sovereignty in the hell of a concentration camp. What formed the diamond-hard character of these women? The forging furnace of God's providence, both before the war and during it. These two women's experiences are indivisible from each other. In the next two chapters, we will look at both Betsie and Corrie and what they overcame – first, their singleness, and then the great potential for bitterness in their lives, over which forgiveness ultimately reigned.

So much of old Haarlem ran on tradition. The ancient rambling buildings, the huge cherry tree called the 'Bride of Haarlem' for its magnificent blossoms, the canals which reminded the local Hollanders how the land itself had been reclaimed from sea and swamp. Casper ten Boom's tiny, rickety watch shop was an institution in Haarlem; it had been established by Casper's grandfather fifty years ago, and would last another fifty. Casper and his wife were also institutions. Casper was beloved amongst the village children for his love and kindness, and his wife was known for the soup pot and knitting that flew all over town into every poor or suffering household. Regulated in all his ways, you could set your clock by the time Casper took the huge family Bible down from its shelf after dinner, to lead family devotions with anyone who happened to be around his table – friends, business competitors, foster children.

Betsie was the first child born into this happy, godly home. But from an early age, it seemed clear that she was destined not to follow in her mother's footsteps as a homemaker. She suffered from pernicious anaemia, a condition which meant she could never bear children. While it's common these days to see all different kinds of families, Betsie saw that she could not fulfil her idea of what a wife and mother should be in the late nineteenth century. It would not be fair to begin a relationship with a man knowing that she could never give him his own children. Betsie decided she would never marry. As far as we know, it was a resolution in which she never wavered.

Corrie, younger by seven years, was the opposite of her sister in almost every way. Where Betsie was elegant, Corrie was ramshackle. Where Betsie was refined and decorous, Corrie was bustling and tenacious. Where Betsie was delicate, Corrie was adventurous. And where Betsie carefully trained her emotions away from romantic entanglements, Corrie fell in love hard.

She was fourteen when she first laid eyes on Karel, who was studying theology alongside her big brother Willem. Karel was handsome, blond, and the six years he had over her in age was enough to be exotic but not unreachable. After that first meeting her attraction to him simmered in the background, and seeing him again a few years later, she was awestruck to find that he remembered her. He seemed to like her and wanted to know about her interests. Their friendship grew slowly, and long solitary walks gave opportunity to discuss Karel's future – which they soon started to discuss, casually, as *their* future.

It was then that Willem told Corrie that Karel could never marry her. He would have a marriage arranged for him by his parents, who had set their hearts on his marrying 'well'. Wishing to please his mother, he was not free to court a poor clockmaker's daughter, however respectable.

Though heartbroken at this dashing of her hopes and of finding Karel had not acted honourably toward her, Corrie did not really let go of her desire – not until a few months later, when Karel showed up at the little house in Haarlem to introduce his bride-to-be. Corrie remembered that half-hour visit as a nightmarish montage: her family doing their best to carry the conversation and serve the refreshments, so that she could concentrate on hiding her feelings, until at last the happy couple left and she could flee to her room.

How long I lay on my bed sobbing for the one love of my life I do not know. Later, I heard Father's footsteps coming up the stairs...suddenly I was afraid of what Father would say. Afraid he would say, 'There'll be someone else soon,' and that forever afterward this untruth would lie between us. For in some deep part of me I knew already that there would not – soon or ever – be anyone else.

The sweet cigar-smell came into the room with Father. And of course he did not say the false, idle words.

'Corrie,' he began instead, 'do you know what hurts so very much? It's love. Love is the strongest force in the world, and when it is blocked that means pain.

'...God loves Karel – even more than you do – and if you ask Him, He will give you His love for this man, a love nothing can prevent, nothing destroy. Whenever we cannot love in the old, human way, Corrie, God can give us the perfect way.'[1]

After her father left, Corrie was finally able to pray: 'Lord, I give to You the way I feel about Karel, my thoughts about our future – oh, You know! Everything! Give me Your way of seeing Karel instead. Help me to love him that way. That much.'

After surviving the Holocaust, she reflected: 'I did not know...that he had put into my hands the secret that would open far darker rooms than this – places where there was not, on a human level, anything to love at all.'[2]

Years passed. Corrie and Betsie's beloved mother suffered a stroke which left her paralyzed, but even in her infirmity she demonstrated a powerful lesson on how to love others well. This was a woman who had been famous for her hospitality

---

1   Corrie ten Boom, *The Hiding Place*, (London: Hodder & Stoughton, 1972), p. 46. Copyright © 2015 Corrie Ten Boom. Reproduced by permission of Hodder Faith.

2   Ibid.

– but, without her hands and feet to serve others, Corrie's Mama instead sat at the window and watched people, praying for those who passed by, for those in the house who so gently tended her, for cities and nations she could not see. Her love for others seemed to grow, not diminish, in her infirmity.

There was a third ten Boom sister, Nollie, the only one to marry. It was at her wedding that God gave Mrs ten Boom a great gift – he opened her mouth and allowed her to sing to his glory. At her favourite hymn being played, the dear paralyzed lady could suddenly sing every word. She had not spoken for years, except for yes, no, and Corrie's name – the last word she had said before falling into a coma, it seemed to have been burned into her brain – and, after this hymn, she never spoke again; in fact, she died a few weeks later. It was characteristic of Mrs ten Boom that she bore no bitterness against the Lord for the hard providence of her paralysis, but instead rejoiced that she was allowed once more to sing His praise!

But it was also during this wedding that Corrie herself received a gift from the Lord. This was her freedom from her 'old' love for Karel. As she watched her sister walk down the aisle with her new husband, Corrie suddenly remembered how much she had longed for a wedding with Karel. Now she and Betsie shared a pew, well past the usual marrying age of that time.

> I knew that this was the way it was going to be: Betsie and I the unmarried daughters living at home in the Beje.
>
> It was a happy thought, not a sad one. And that was the moment when I knew for sure that God had accepted the faltering gift of my emotions made four years ago. For

with the thought of Karel – all shining round with love as thoughts of him had been since I was fourteen – came not the slightest trace of hurt.[3]

Years ticked by, and the household fell into a pattern. Corrie became a clockmaker herself, and kept the shop's books; Betsie served the whole town with an open door and an ever-simmering coffee and soup pot, just as her mother had done before her. Casper read the family devotions every night at 8:45. Nollie's and Willem's children arrived and grew. The family were involved in the Reformed Church, and Corrie led a worship service for mentally disabled people.

In 1937, the clock shop held its 100th birthday party, and the shop and the house above it were crammed full of people to honour Casper, the 'Grand Old Man of Haarlem', and his daughters. That morning Corrie was struck that she had only three places to lay at the table. There were no aged aunts living with them, no foster children, no Willem or Nollie or Mama. The house had never been so empty...

In a way it was inevitable that, when the war started in earnest and Holland fell, the ten Booms would become a landing-place for every desperate Jew, disabled person and Resistance worker in Haarlem. They had always had an open door to anyone in need or confusion; they could not conceive of any other life. For a while they simply put people up for a night or two on their way to a home in the countryside or a quieter part of the Netherlands, arranging ration cards and extra clothes for the journey, but eventually they found a niche

---

3   Ibid., p. 51.

of people all their own. A man with blatantly stereotypical Jewish features, a woman with a noisy asthmatic wheeze – in other words, the people whom others did not want to take in. The rejects of society were those that the ten Booms chose to love. Those were the people that became their new family.

After two years running the Underground from their tiny house, the ten Booms were arrested and sent to concentration camps, initially in the Netherlands and then in Germany. Casper died after ten days, but Corrie and Betsie were imprisoned for months – and struck, starved, frozen, neglected, subjected to solitary confinement, and crowded into flea-infested barracks with hundreds of other women.

The huge family that had once filled the little house over the shop had now contracted to two middle-aged women in striped overalls. Yet, Corrie was grateful that her parents were not alive to experience this torture ('Had I really cried for my father?' she wonders, seeing the brutality that he was missing), and more grateful for Betsie's company. And she saw that those with larger families were often simply subjected to more suffering. The wives and mothers in the camp searched anxiously for a glimpse of their men as they marched past, all identical in prison uniform. Every time shots rang out across the camp – for the men's side was much more prone to violent discipline – the women died a little too, wondering if this time it had been their husband or son.

With no husbands or children to worry about, and no control over the fates of those still on the outside whom they loved, the sisters set about building a new family yet again – right there in the camp. If there were hundreds of women crowded into their barracks, then hundreds of women were going to hear that the good news of Jesus was for them too; yes, even in the hell of Vught or Ravensbruck, Jesus' hope and love and salvation would make sisters and mothers and daughters of these persecuted strangers. And when the war was over, that good news would go on to turn even their persecutors and betrayers into brothers and friends.

> *I appeal to you therefore, brothers, by the mercies of God, to present your bodies as a living sacrifice, holy and acceptable to God, which is your spiritual worship. Do not be conformed to this world, but be transformed by the renewal of your mind, that by testing you may discern what is the will of God, what is good and acceptable and perfect.* (Rom. 12:1-2, ESV)

Singleness: Problem or Blessing?

Many churches seem to view their single people, particularly the younger ones, as being in a sort of waiting room, subject to matchmaking, focused prayer and exhortations to patience: 'It'll happen one day.' One wonders what Betsie and Corrie would have made of such remarks and strategies! It is striking that, where singleness might not have been their preferred choice, they nevertheless took care to fully reconcile and dedicate themselves to it. They 'owned' their lifestyle. It is also striking how full and happy their lives were, not in spite of singleness, but because of it. The world and the Church need more women like the ten Boom sisters.

Whether we are single, wives, mums, widows, or career-oriented, we all live with unfulfilled desires and plans to which we can't find the answer. How can we all deal with the longing of our hearts?

God's promises and plan for the single

Is God still good? Why won't He provide the one thing I really need to be happy?

Throughout the Bible, some of God's chiefest promises to us are that He is on our side (Ps. 118:6); has plans to prosper us, not to harm us (Jer. 29:11 NIV); and holds nothing back from His children that would truly benefit them ('He who did not spare his own Son...how will he not also with him graciously give us all things?' [Rom. 8:32, ESV]). One of the hardest verses in Scripture to truly understand, for me, is John 14:14 (ESV): 'If you ask me anything in my name, I will do it.' *Anything?* So often we distrust this prayer because we ask for so much that we do not receive. James 4:3 (ESV) gives us the answer to this conundrum: 'You ask and do not receive, because you ask wrongly, to spend it on your passions.'

That verse might make us wince just a little. We ask for things that seem good, noble, wholesome in our own eyes. But do we really ask them in Jesus' name – i.e. asking what we believe would enable us to give Him greater glory and service? Or might we give Him greater glory when we are contented, joyful and praise-filled even when we don't have the earthly lifestyle or family we desire?

If you have been single and in the church for a while, you may well have a love-hate relationship with Paul's words on marriage. Here's *The Message* translation of 1 Corinthians 7:17, 32-35:

> *And don't be wishing you were someplace else or with someone else. Where you are right now is God's place for you. Live and obey and love and believe right there. God, not your marital status, defines your life. Don't think I'm being harder on you than on the others. I give this same counsel in all the churches. ...I want you to live as free of complications as possible. When you're unmarried, you're free to concentrate on simply pleasing the Master. Marriage involves you in all the nuts and bolts of domestic life and in wanting to please your spouse, leading to so many more demands on your attention. The time and energy that married people spend on caring for and nurturing each other, the unmarried can spend in becoming whole and holy instruments of God. I'm trying to be helpful and make it as easy as possible for you, not make things harder. All I want is for you to be able to develop a way of life in which you can spend plenty of time together with the Master without a lot of distractions.*

Now, of course, much of the time we love distractions and positively welcome them! That's our weakness. But what Paul is really offering is permission to inhabit any sphere of life to the glory of God, contentedly and single-mindedly, and not with the definitions of worth that the world clings to. In fact, earlier in the chapter, Paul says he wishes all people could be content in singleness, as he is, because he takes so much satisfaction in Christ that it completely fills him up.

Rather than leaving this section with Paul's reassuring but somewhat daunting advice, I'd like to bring out a special promise that, at first sight, may look rather unexpected.

> *He was giving them the very best – a place of abiding in Himself.*

'And the Lord said to Aaron, "You shall have no inheritance in their land, neither shall you have any portion among them. I am your portion and your inheritance among the people of Israel"' (Num. 18:20, ESV). While doling out portions of the Promised Land to the various tribes of Israel, God is here telling Aaron, the High Priest and the leader of the Levites, the tribe of priests, that they don't get one. What! These were the dedicated servants of the Lord. Why didn't they deserve at least as much of the blessing as everyone else?

But, of course, what the Lord was offering them was far more than land to build their houses. He was giving them the very best – a place of abiding in Himself. They were to trust in Him to provide everything for them, and He would give them a place before His very presence. He would be their *everything*, and they would be filled.

For Christians, a 'nation of priests', the Lord is our portion and inheritance. Yet I think this promise has a special place for those who have no 'portion' to call their own on this earth. How often I look at my tiny bit of land (well, my garden), and my home, and my family, to give me security! Instead of looking at the Lord who actually sustains me. Are

> *are we waiting well?...Or do we put our happiness, trust, and fruitfulness on hold until we get the thing that we want most?*

you looking for an earthly inheritance, or are you living out your right to inhabit the very presence of the Lord?

Are you waiting?

The fact is that many of us spend much of our lives waiting – not just for marriage, but for career progression, financial security, children, grandchildren, retirement, better health. In one respect there is nothing wrong with waiting. We are not in control of our lives, and we are always waiting to see what God has in store for us. But are we waiting well? Are we waiting in submission to His will, praising Him in the meantime and carrying out His work in the world? Or do we put our happiness, trust, and fruitfulness on hold until we get the thing that we want most?

There is, of course, a temptation to date non-believers if no Christian prospects are forthcoming. Relationships with non-Christians don't always lead to an abandonment of faith, but they do make practicing your faith much, much harder than it would be with someone who shared it. A Christian who starts a relationship with a non-believer both discourages and enables other single Christians who face the same temptations. It also prevents you from having a husband who is able to model spiritual headship and build you up in Christ. And, frankly, marriage is hard enough when both people share the same point of reference: a biblical moral code and a mutual submission to Christ. When two people have completely different moral authorities, it is difficult to reach any real understanding, and communication is infinitely harder. The Bible says that light can have no fellowship with darkness.[4] Someone who belongs to Jesus lives in the light. Someone who puts their trust in the things of this world, whether in materialism or ambition or their own philosophical ideas, is in darkness. Don't live your life in this twilight, out of unwillingness to wait on the Lord.

Are you complete?

The term 'my other half' is particularly unhelpful for single Christians. While a biblical marriage does indeed mean becoming one flesh, physically and spiritually yoked together, it does not follow that a Christian without a spouse is therefore

> *...no one (single or married) can be complete but in a relationship with Him.*

less of a Christian or a person. As Corrie noted in the concentration camp, the married women also seemed to carry double the burden of the single prisoners, as they feared for their husbands. That's an extreme example, but it's true that, while married women have their spouses to help carry their burdens, they also bear those of their husbands.

Neither does marriage put a full stop to that feeling of incompletion. Once married, wives seek completeness not through finding a husband, but through maintaining the marriage, and often look for emotional fulfilment not in the Lord but in their husbands' attention.

Marriage is hard work, and many fail; and for 'marriage', substitute all human relationships. Children will disappoint

---

4   2 Corinthians 6:14.

us, parents will leave us, friends will grow apart. Christ is the only one who will always nurture us, always be faithful and predictable, always give joy and peace and good counsel to those who ask Him. He is the only one who can complete us. And, in fact, since we were created to glorify and commune with God, no one (single or married) can be complete *but* in a relationship with Him.

Are you looking?

'I'm still looking for the right one. I haven't found him yet!' Well, there's no harm in looking – is there? Do you see single Christian men more in terms of their boyfriend potential than their potential for Christ's kingdom? Are you tempted to flirt with many of the men at church, or go out with guys even when you don't see a future for the relationship?

We are all tempted to see people in terms of what they can give us instead of how we can work together for God. We all look around at church and see those who share our passion for rugby, those who have a holiday home we might be able to use this summer, those who can help with DIY, those who always remember to take an interest in our affairs and pray for us – and those that seem like perfectly upstanding Christians but really hold no interest for us. The handsome people and the unattractive, the fabulous and the irritating. We need to love *all* of these people in God's way, seeking their good and looking for how we can live at one for His kingdom. Instead of looking for romantic potential, be on the lookout for people's spiritual gifts, and for their needs.

So, are you looking with Jesus' eyes? Are you looking for ways to foster 1 Corinthians 13 love – the love Corrie eventually felt for Karel – which is patient with the pushy, keeps no record of wrongs against those who do us much wrong, and always thinks the best of others?

Can you help the way you feel?

One of the more overlooked fruits of the Spirit might be self-control, or self-discipline. It's true that we don't invite some feelings in. But do we nurture and indulge them even when it seems clear that God's will is not to further the relationship? Or, if in a relationship, do we compromise on our honesty, sincerity, or purity in order to please our partner?

I see three main temptations to let our feelings take control. The first is the inclination to despondency and disappointment in God because we are lonely or unfulfilled. Focusing on these feelings takes your eyes off Jesus and puts them on yourself – and, like Peter, you just sink further. Seeking Jesus through the sadness, telling Him of your longings and even your frustration (see the book of Psalms!) draws you closer to Him. One of these feeds and enlarges your misery; the other consoles and soothes it. Which do you choose?

The second is a temptation to obsess over a particular man who takes your fancy. The fancy may not leave you, but don't give anyone too much space in your head who doesn't belong there. This is not easy, I know. But when you find yourself fantasizing about your future, even about the next time you'll see a particular man, stop yourself and ask if it's helpful. Now, I know there's a frisson of excitement and anticipation when you meet someone you like. And it's delightful! But train yourself to pray for that person like a brother, and leave the relationship in God's hands, not feeding it with your thoughts until a happy wish becomes an all-consuming desire. Corrie was so practiced with this that eventually her longing for Karel morphed into an innocent reminiscence that comforted her in a labour camp: 'Sweet summer smells came in the breezes for the farms around the camp; sometimes I would dream that Karel and I were walking hand in hand along a country lane.' She loved him so much in Christ's way that the memory of her old feelings for her posed no threat, no tension, no unrequited longing. They were, in a sense, redeemed.

Finally, there is sexual temptation. Fantasies, pornography and masturbation seem such harmless sins, chiefly because they are seldom exposed. We can easily excuse secret sins to ourselves. But it is absolutely true that making what should be an expression of mutual love into a selfish animal pleasure corrupts the soul, leads us into guilt and shame, and drives us further from Christ. Don't get into selfish sexual habits; they are hard to break. Rosaria Butterfield gives good advice on allowing sin no quarter in the chapter on homosexuality.

Are you expecting too much – or too little?

Don't I have a right to expect what everyone else seems to get so easily? The Bible speaks very little about our rights in life. It commands us to uphold others' rights – by acting justly and honestly – but otherwise, the good things that do come to us in life are all through grace: God's favour coming upon those who don't deserve it! So often we sabotage our own happiness with our expectations of what our lives will look like, one day, when everything is sorted. The popular term for this now is FOMO – Fear of Missing Out. We are also, these days, very much interested in our 'rights'. Having a husband and family just seem like what we are entitled to expect out of life.

But don't forget that what Christ offers us is never just 'normal'. His promises in the Bible are never for others to desire us, or for an average worldly life, or for prosperity. Instead He promises abundance. 'I came that they may have life, and have it abundantly.'[5] He promises extraordinary spiritual power, the indwelling of the Holy Spirit as our Comforter, a family of countless fellow-believers, eternal life, victory, joy, strength, His constant presence and help. I could go on and on. We often scorn these things in favour of our greatest earthly desires. We have heard the verses, but we don't *expect* abundance, power, joy. Let's seek these things first – in faith and expectation – and all the earthly provision we need will be added to us; but I suspect that if we truly inhabited these promises, we would have much less interest in the temporal blessings we spend so much time seeking.

Are you enough?

What's wrong with me – why doesn't anyone want me? Long singleness comes with the danger of low self-esteem. We are all tempted to see our value in terms of how wanted, admired and needed we are by other people. But our use to God, or our worthiness or beauty in His sight, is never affected by

---

5   John 10:10, ESV.

Live with the default position that God has already placed you within His will

how other people see us. In that respect, we are always alone before Him – even in marriage. We have already noted in previous chapters that there is 'no marriage in heaven' – our relationships from earth pale into insignificance compared to our view of Christ. No one will be more precious or enjoyable or attractive to us than He will. We won't look for our fulfilment anywhere else, or compromise on any aspect of our holiness for the sake of other people. Let's live in that 'heavenly' place now.

And don't forget the power, so evident in the ten Boom sisters, of owning their singleness. They took great care to accept their place in life, stop waiting, and simply live their best life doing the work before them and enjoying God's blessings around them. Live with the default position that God has already placed you within His will, and while He further conforms you to Jesus' character each day, you are already whole and complete in Him. Your circumstances can add absolutely nothing to that.

Can I still bear fruit?

You are in a unique place to dedicate yourself to Christ for as long as He gives you the space, freedom, quiet and opportunities of singleness. And if you foster in yourself cheerfulness, contentment, gratitude and a faithful pursuit of the Lord, you will be a magnificent testimony to the entire Church as well as to the world. Time is passing, regardless of your attitude, and it is in the Lord's hand to give you a spouse, or not. So steward the time well. You'll be happier, more fruitful, and you will find the family you need among God's people. None of these characteristics are things we can achieve for ourselves, in the midst of a genuine sadness and loneliness. Spread your feelings before the Lord as Hezekiah spread his letter.[6] Confess where you are struggling to see Him as the greatest good, as your portion, and ask Him with an open heart to fill all the emptiness. Let Him do the hard work in you, and you will never, ever regret it.

Questions

1. What are your greatest unfulfilled desires? Are they things that distract you from serving and praising God?
2. In what ways is the Lord your 'portion' – fulfilling you where earthly relationships can't? What other empty places in your life would you like Him to fill, and what might that look like?
3. Is there discontentment or impurity that you need to repent of?

All to Jesus I surrender:
All to him I freely give.
I will ever love and trust him
In his Presence daily live.

---

6   2 Kings 19 – King Hezekiah of Judah receives a letter from the Assyrian king threatening to lay waste to Jerusalem. Knowing he can't fight this superior power, Hezekiah takes the letter into God's temple and simply lays it before Him. God hears the king's prayer of trust and miraculously destroys the Assyrian army.

I surrender all, I surrender all;
All to thee, my precious Saviour,
I surrender all.
—Judson W. Van DeVenter

5 Overcoming with Forgiveness
Betsie & Corrie ten Boom

Corrie ten Boom had something of the Apostle Peter's character about her, with his strength, and also a touch of his pugnaciousness! She remembered her father's main business competitor, Mr Kan, dropping into the shop on 'social calls' – really to find out how much her father was charging for particular watches that he could undersell them! When she pointed this out to her father, he was merely delighted to hear that the locals would be able to get their products for a lower price than he could sell at. Mr Kan was always treated as a special guest, Corrie's warnings notwithstanding.

Betsie reflected perfectly her father's generous perspective of people whom Corrie quite naturally viewed as the 'enemy'. There was no one who was too great a call on her resources, no time or generosity she resented giving to others. Anyone who reflects this sacrificial aspect of Christ's person eventually attracts attention, and Corrie first noted this characteristic in her sister on the night that the German bombing started over Holland. In the midst of the roaring plane engines and the shaking of the explosives, she and Betsie knelt down and prayed for hours for Holland and for those who were suffering through the night.

> And then, incredibly, Betsie began to pray for the Germans, up there in the planes, caught in the fist of the giant evil loose in Germany. I looked at my sister kneeling beside me in the light of burning Holland. 'Oh Lord,' I whispered, 'listen to Betsie, not me, because I cannot pray for those men at all.'[1]

It was then that Corrie experienced her first vision – a vivid sight of herself, along with her family, sitting on a truck in the main square of Haarlem, being taken somewhere they did not want to go. Although it was troubling, Betsie reminded her that, if it were a vision indeed, God had given it to strengthen and not to frighten her.

As the war continued and the Nazis' persecution of Jews and other minorities grew more and more brazen, Corrie was horrified. Her father and sister were too, but for a different reason – their extraordinary compassion for their enemies. Corrie cried out with sorrow for those who were being taken away from their homes, but her father's grief lay elsewhere. 'Those poor people,' Father echoed. But to my surprise I saw that he was looking at the soldiers now forming into ranks to march away. 'I pity the poor Germans, Corrie. They have touched the apple of God's eye.'[2]

If it seemed that Father and Betsie could afford to be lavish with their sympathy toward the Nazis when the violence was

---

1   *The Hiding Place,* p. 63.

2   Ibid., p. 69.

aimed at other people, they had a chance to prove themselves soon enough. When the family was arrested, Corrie exclaimed with horror that Betsie's face had been beaten by an officer. Betsie merely said, 'I feel so sorry for him.'[3]

Betsie and Corrie were, mercifully, allowed to remain together at their second concentration camp and even had a Bible smuggled to them. Over and over again, during their imprisonment, Corrie saw and marvelled at Betsie's love and compassion for her persecutors. Where Corrie longed to provide a place for prisoners to heal and grow, Betsie could think of nothing but giving the same to their captors.

'Corrie, if people can be taught to hate, they can be taught to love! We must find the way, you and I, no matter how long it takes,' Betsie told her sister excitedly. As she was speaking, Corrie glanced around the room and noticed the matron who was so cruel to them. She realised that her vision was very different from her sister's: 'I saw a gray uniform and a visored hat: Betsie saw a wounded human being.'[4]

Corrie herself had a much harder time forgiving her captors and, most of all, the fellow countryman who had betrayed her household to the Nazis. One of the greatest temptations of her spiritual life came the day that she heard his name: it was the temptation to hate. And, for a time, Corrie indulged it fully. She became obsessed with his name, Jan Vogel: the most horrifying, contemptible name in the world to her. She imagined her father dying alone in a hallway – because of Jan

---

3   Ibid., p. 125.

4   Ibid., pp. 164-165.

Vogel. One of her dear refugees that she had hidden in her home had been arrested – because of Jan Vogel. She and Betsie were in this hell-on-earth – because of Jan Vogel. She wanted to kill him.

Unsurprisingly, while Corrie dwelled on her hatred, she found it impossible to lead devotions in the barracks. She felt sick and couldn't sleep. And why was it that Betsie seemed as peaceful as ever, totally undisturbed? Finally Corrie had to ask.

> 'Betsie, don't you feel anything about Jan Vogel? Doesn't it bother you?'
> 'Oh yes, Corrie! Terribly! I've felt for him ever since I knew – and pray for him whenever his name comes into my mind. How dreadfully he must be suffering.'[5]

Betsie went to sleep, but Corrie lay awake again, convicted of her own terrible sin – of murder. She had hated the man and would hate him even to death if she had the power. Was her sin any better than that traitor's? Suddenly she knew it was not.

> 'Lord Jesus,' I whispered into the lumpy ticking of the bed, 'I forgive Jan Vogel as I pray that You will forgive me. I have done him great damage. Bless him now, and his family...'[6]

During their few months at Ravensbruck, as Betsie's health declined, she began to describe to Corrie an enormous, beautiful house they would one day run for the benefit of the

5   Ibid., p. 169.
6   Ibid.

Nazis' victims, with inlaid wood floors and high ceilings and huge windows. They would transform a concentration camp too, painting it in bright, cheery green, with window boxes and gardens for the residents to help them heal – for those who had been informers and guards. When Corrie questioned whether they would ever be free to start such work, Betsie assured her that they would both be free by the end of the year. On every point, it turned out, Betsie had received a word from the Lord. She was released through a peaceful death in mid-December; Corrie was given her freedom just after Christmas.

As she spoke throughout Holland about her experiences, Corrie was gifted the use of Bloemenhaal, 'one of the most beautiful houses in Holland', for the use of the Nazis' victims, and later she was able to rent a small concentration camp at Darmstadt to minister to those who felt scarred by their country's persecution of others. In the Beje, Corrie's own dear home above the clock shop, she housed informers just like Jan Vogel, who had become social pariahs, hated by all. Now there was yet another new family in that loving home, one formed not by blood but only by the Gospel.

In Bloemenhaal, the prisoners' proximity to one another aided their painful healing; they saw that others had suffered as badly as they themselves. And in every single case, the path to their healing and peace was forgiveness of those who had harmed them the most. As with Corrie herself, it was often the Dutch people who had betrayed their countrymen who were the hardest to forgive.

Instead of nagging people into forgiveness, Corrie used a solution that Betsie had suggested: gardening. As they worked with vegetables and flowers, the residents talked about their pain, and listened too as Corrie talked about the loneliness and shame of the NSBers, those who had been traitors in the war.

> When mention of the NSBers no longer brought on a volley of self-righteous wrath, I knew the person's healing was not far away. And the day he said, 'Those people you spoke of – I wonder if they'd care for some home-grown carrots,' then I knew the miracle had taken place.[7]

There was still one more trial Corrie had to face before her own 'miracle' had fully taken place. This was the day when, speaking at a church service about her experiences, one of her own prison guards – one who had watched and laughed when she and her beloved sister had had to strip naked for medical exams and stand shivering in the long, cold corridor – approached her and, smiling, reached out to shake her hand. He was a brother now in Christ, and yet Corrie felt physically unable to raise her hand. She breathed a silent prayer: 'Jesus, I cannot forgive him. Give me Your forgiveness.' Jesus gave her not only the ability to reach out to the man, but an overwhelming sense of love and sisterhood for him. 'And so I discovered that it is not on our forgiveness that the world's healing hinges, but on His. When He tells us to love our enemies, He gives, along with the command, the love itself.'[8]

> *Be kind to one another, tenderhearted, forgiving one another, as God in Christ forgave you.* (Eph. 4:32, ESV)

---

7   Ibid., p. 220.

8   Ibid., pp. 220-21

What was Betsie's secret?

Corrie ten Boom struggled to forgive. She herself testified that her natural feelings tended to bitterness and rage. But her experience of Betsie was exclusively one of overflowing grace and concern for her persecutors. What was it that made Betsie so sacrificially loving? Both sisters were raised by parents that exhibited selflessness both in their generosity and their attitudes. Both were highly spiritual women who knew the Bible inside out and ran their own spheres of ministry. Both had seen God's miraculous provision for them particularly in the years of their underground activity.

I believe Betsie's singleness was one of the major elements that made her so Christlike. She knew she would never have a husband and children on her own, and by the time of war, many of the people who had once filled her home had died. She therefore had long experience of casting her whole lot on the Lord – finding in Him every contentment, every need fulfilled, every security for her future. Her thorn in the flesh – anaemia – meant that she felt her weakness acutely, but rather than focusing on that, she chose to turn her eyes to Christ and inhabit His strength.

Seeing how He filled every crevice and corner of her life, she could not but be horrified and sorry for those who were utterly separated from Him. She also exhibited a forgiveness toward others that only comes from someone who knows just how greatly they have been saved – though living an outwardly upright life, Betsie was no doubt deeply aware of the many inward sins that Christ had saved her from, and wanted to extend that salvation to others.

While many Christians are forgiving people, there are few as open, free and loving as this fifty-something woman in a Nazi concentration camp. Her capacity can only be truly explained by a special outpouring of grace given her by the Holy Spirit, who used her to point Corrie back to Himself and uses her even now to give us a picture of what it looks like to follow in Christ's footsteps. For Betsie's example was not other Christians and their ability to forgive, but Christ alone, who had prayed compassionately, even while dying, that God forgive His ignorant murderers. Through following His example, Betsie took part in Christ's sufferings.

Why do we forgive?

It can be tempting to look at the ten Booms' story and say, 'I could forgive these lost people who have done such terrible things – I could be persecuted for Christ's sake. But Betsie didn't have to forgive that person in my own church who spread gossip about me!'

it's very often the small and insignificant and petty things that Satan uses to drive a wedge between us and other people

And the truth is, it's very often the small and insignificant and petty things that Satan uses to drive a wedge between us and other people, even other Christians. That niggling hurt at what someone said, or the promise they didn't keep, or the service they didn't appreciate, can, if indulged, spread its poison over an entire relationship, and spread outward to families, social circles, whole congregations or denominations. 'How great a forest is set ablaze by such a small fire!' James exclaims in chapter 3:5 (ESV), speaking of our words. Forgiveness is the water that puts out the tongue's fire.

How do we forgive?

Corrie shows examples of forgiving both those who asked her forgiveness and those who did not; Betsie exclusively the latter. And it's true that in our lives, the most common occurrence is those who never apologise.

The fact that someone doesn't say sorry is no excuse not to forgive them. But don't make forgiveness easy by just deciding in your own mind it 'doesn't matter' – the Bible's model doesn't only give guidance that someone who has offended their friend should go and seek forgiveness, but also that someone who *has been* offended should go to their friend and tell them of the offence.

To paper over an offence while still feeling the pain of it and treating the person as if nothing has happened is dishonest and eats away at the foundation of the relationship – trust and openness. There may be times when a full, practical reconciliation is not possible: when the other party is not traceable, for example, or if they are unwilling to listen or to understand your hurt. How to deal with such situations is complex and depends on the relationship. The world tells us to keep our distance from those who have hurt us, to guard ourselves from further pain. There are times when that is necessary, especially where there is abuse or risk of harm. But the Bible's guidance is to follow the problem through to the end – at least where the offence has occurred within the church body.

> *If your brother sins against you, go and tell him his fault, between you and him alone. If he listens to you, you have gained your brother. But if he does not listen, take one or two others along with you, that every charge may be established by the evidence of two or three witnesses. If he refuses to listen to them, tell it to the church. And if he refuses to listen even to the church, let him be to you as a Gentile and a tax collector.* (Matt. 18:15-17, ESV)

Following this process through to its conclusion may end up with a real break in the relationship, or a renewal of it. This is even harder with family – parents, spouses, children – where a complete break is not possible. There are times to let 'love cover a multitude of sins',[9] and there are times to confront a frequent offender even if it risks the peace of the home or community.

And there are many times when we are still growing in discernment; when we struggle to know whether to meet a situation with sympathy or firmness; when we can't see clearly where fault lies, and when to start a difficult conversation, and what words to use. There are times when we sin in our anger or our weakness or our lack of understanding. There are times when we simply cry out to the Lord for wisdom and grace when our own poor resources are utterly depleted.

At such times it is humbling, and a relief, to know firsthand just how patient God is with us. 'He remembers that

---

9   1 Peter 4:8, ESV.

we are dust';[10] He knows we are only babies before Him and have no wisdom or strength of our own. He knows that our understanding grows through experience, and even as we may be seeking Him all along our path, it is sometimes only well down the road that the miles we've travelled start to make sense to us, and we look back and see our wrong turns and false starts. He forgives us so much, even when we have taken step after step in the wrong direction.

When we see His patience with us, it's easier to forgive others their own wanderings – and, to misquote Tolkien's famous phrase, so often those who wander *are* lost. Can we see, from our own tiring and rocky road, that the person who has grievously sinned against us is stuck in the mud in a terrifying dark forest? Through grace and forgiveness, can we offer them a light back to the right path by pointing them back to Jesus? And not by making an apology our condition of help, but by being vulnerable

Uriah was simply an object in the way of a man who had come to see himself as not only king but also god of his own life.

enough to show them our hurt and our loving willingness to restore the relationship so that we may walk side by side toward heaven.

10   Psalm 103:14.

How to encourage someone toward repentance rather than apology

While apologies are aimed toward other people, repentance is offered to God. It is only recently that I really understood David's admission, 'Against you, you only, have I sinned.'[11] David had seduced a man's wife and then had him killed! Surely he had sinned against Uriah as well as God?! But in fact, Uriah was only the recipient of David's bad fruit, the result of his selfish heart. David's attitudes, his entitlement, his lust, his ruthlessness, were all offenses against a God who had made man to worship and enjoy Himself. Every terrible action David took was in direct disobedience to God's commands and insulting to God's goodness. Uriah was simply an object in the way of a man who had come to see himself as not only king but also god of his own life. And, royalty or not, we have all been there. We have all entertained impure thoughts. We have all been angry enough to just wish someone away from us – wish them out of our life. We have all turned our shoulder to God and nursed petty thoughts in our cold hearts. Against Him, Him only, have we sinned.

In the same way, those who sin against us may hurt us, emotionally or physically, but it is really God they are disobeying. Our pain is simply a consequence of their offense against Him. We should be honest when we are deeply pained by someone's actions or cruel words, but if we are only interested in an apology for breaking *our* rules – *love*

---

11   Psalm 51:4. The story of David, Bathsheba and Uriah is found in 2 Samuel 11.

OVERCOMING WITH FORGIVENESS

me, be kind to me, give me the respect I need – then, again, we are confusing ourselves with God. And the apology and the change will be shallow, because true reconciliation and renewal only comes with repentance before God.

I am not suggesting you go to your friend or spouse and say, 'Look at this verse. It plainly shows that what you did to me was wrong in God's eyes. You'd better talk to *Him* about it!'

Instead I suggest the following:

1. *Examine yourself for the beam in your own eye.*[12] If your attitude is that of proving to someone that they are in the wrong and you are in the right, your approach will be a confrontation and you will both be defensive. If you are a much-forgiven fellow traveller on the road to glory, willing to own your own faults, you will approach them with compassion and concern for their own wellbeing.

2. *Present the situation in terms of your vulnerability, not their wrongdoing.* 'I felt hurt that I wasn't included in the meeting,' not 'You should have invited me – what happened?'

3. *Listen.* Is it a woman thing that we run the scenario so many times in our head before a difficult conversation that it is hard to go off-script when it's happening in real life? Sometimes I feel like one of those telesales operators who look at a computer screen giving them dialogue options depending on their customer's last answer! Do we ask our friend or loved one questions really wanting to know how they feel, or just as a bridge to get to our next point?

---

12 Matthew 7:5.

4. *Allow space and Spirit.* To adapt a phrase, you can point someone to Christ but you can't make them repent. Humbly lay before them your concerns. If they need time to think about it, that's fine. Sometimes people have to process a conversation and let the Holy Spirit work through it. Pray earnestly for their spiritual eyes to be opened and heart to be softened. Offer kindness and patience. If they won't repent, and the relationship is otherwise too wounded to continue, then it may be time to seek mediation

There is no freedom without forgiveness.

with an elder, minister or Christian counsellor. If they come back to you, 'you have won your brother'.

None of this is easy. It is only through God's wisdom, strength and grace we can do it at all. But it is worth remembering that holding on to anger hurts us far more than the other person. There is no freedom without forgiveness.

How do we know when we have forgiven?

There are times when we have had a heart-to-heart with someone who has offended us, and have reached a conclusion. Apologies have been offered and accepted, or at least explanations have been made. But our feelings haven't changed. We still feel wounded and not particularly interested in the other person's company or welfare. What next?

First, it's true that time really does a lot of healing work. Sometimes we have to let the matter rest until we can pick up the friendship again or spend Christmas with that particular sibling or parent! And that's okay. Sometimes we have to formally forgive first, in obedience to God, and let the feelings follow.

I know I have forgiven someone when I can pray, as Corrie did, for their good. Not just pray that they would be brought to repentance – or justice! – but that they would be blessed, would be joyful and peaceful, would prosper.

There have been times when I've reached a formal understanding with someone only to truly understand and empathise with them years later, and forge a real reconciliation. It is so joyful to be able to say, 'I now understand what I did to you. Please forgive me. I miss you.' It is one of the blessings of spiritual maturity to receive those friendships back. And there have been times when I knew I could happily meet someone in company again after a fracture, and be interested in their lives and delight in their good news.

But the best gauge is this: what does the Lord's forgiveness toward us look like? It looks like total, cherishing, providing, assuring, delighted acceptance. And that alone should motivate us to show this forgiveness to others, and see them also changed into His image.

Be thankful

Finally, a famous story about the sisters' arrival at their new barracks in Ravensbruck gives a clue as to the secret of Betsie's peace. It was a horrifying place, and the sisters were initially crestfallen upon their arrival in their new barracks. But then Betsie remembered their morning Bible reading. Carefully, Corrie took out their secret Bible to return to the passage. It was 1 Thessalonians 5:18, 'give thanks in all circumstances.' Betsie then compelled an unwilling Corrie to thank God for the rampant fleas in the barracks.

Months later, Corrie arrived back from her day's labour to find Betsie with a twinkle in her eye. She had overheard the guards talking. What was it that had providentially kept them away from the sisters' dorm, giving the complete liberty to lead worship services and read Scripture to hundreds of women? The fleas, of course!

Betsie looked at the world around her – including but not limited to the people – with God's eyes. She saw that all things were under His control, and that she was within His loving shelter. This gave her the security to give thanks, and the emotional bandwidth to look on even the cruellest people with compassion. Corrie was one of those who had the gift of enduring, but Betsie – she overcame. She overcame even unto death.

Can I bear fruit?

One of the verses that frightens me the most in the whole Bible is Matthew 6:15. 'But if you do not forgive others their sins, our Father will not forgive your sins.' This frightens me for myself when I see the bitterness in my own heart. It frightens me for other Christians when I see them bearing grudges too. We need to examine ourselves regularly for offenses that we are holding against others.

Can you bear fruit after being desperately hurt? Without forgiving, I would suggest that genuine spiritual fruit is out of the question. That is because bitterness withers us. It dries us up inside, exhausts our energy, stands in the way of our communion with God – and there is no overflow of life to bloom. This is how bitterness hurts ourselves far more than the person who has offended us. Holding grudges suggests that we have no real concept of our own sin, or of the sacrifice Jesus made to free us from it. But there is good news.

Forgiveness *is* fruit. Forgiveness is sacrifice on a human scale, a living portrayal of the divine sacrifice of our Saviour. 'To err is human, to forgive is divine' is pretty accurate as clichés go. All of us fallen humans sin, but God is the only one who empowers the sacrifice of forgiveness. Isaiah 42:3 prophesied of the Messiah, 'A bruised reed he will not break'. Even if you have started to wither through long bitterness, it is never too late to turn back. Jesus waits so patiently for us, nurturing us through dry spells and gently tending us back to life and fellowship. Can you do the same for others?

Questions

1. Is there anyone in your life that you need to forgive? What beams might there be in your eye that you need to take to the Father before you seek reconciliation?

2. What is a time that you have been extravagantly forgiven – by other people, and by God? How can that motivate you now?

3. In what ways can our forgiveness point others toward Christ? How can you, too, nurture a 'bruised reed'?

And can it be that I should gain
An int'rest in my Saviour's blood?

Died he for me, who caused his pain,
For me, who him to death pursued?
Amazing love! how can it be
That thou, my God, shouldst die for me?
—Charles Wesley

6 Eating Disorders

Christie Dondero Bettwy

Christie is Executive Director of Rock Recovery, a Christian-based organisation which fills gaps in treatment and recovery of eating disorders. For help or further information, see rockrecoveryed.org.

In Her Own Words

I never forgot the first moment I hated my body. It was during a ballet workshop. While giving corrections at the barre, the guest instructor sharply poked my stomach, and declared for the rest of the class to hear that if I didn't want people to think I was a marsupial, I should get rid of my pouch. I was 13. I didn't eat dinner that night, and from that moment on I was no longer concerned with what my body could do or how I treated it. Only with how it looked, and what others thought of it.

A few years later, I found a personal trainer who put me on a strict diet and fitness regimen that was very black and white, and full of rules and regulations. I had a list of 'bad' foods that I couldn't even imagine eating, including some fruits and vegetables that my trainer said 'just had too much sugar'. I was at a very uncertain and unstable time in my life, with my parents moving away and university looming. This new diet and fitness plan really appealed to me because of the loss of stability and lack of control in my wider life. The plan gave me total control over one wonderful thing – my body. What I put into it, and what I did with it. However, this control quickly warped into a critical hatred.

I spent hours in front of the mirror hating my body. Every deviation from stick-thin seemed repulsive. What I initially took on as a means to control my life had turned into something that was somehow controlling me. Surely once my body was perfect, the rest would fall into place: the boyfriend, the grades, the friends, the confidence.

Within six months of graduating college, I had lost and gained weight more times than I could count. I was constantly consumed with counting how many calories I'd eaten in a day, whether it was a 500-calorie starvation diet or a 5,000-calorie binge. I lived in constant fear of what I would eat each day and when I would have time to make it to the gym. I started attending a church after a stranger invited me along, and the pastor's wife made an announcement about a program for anyone struggling with eating disorders, called New ID. *Freedom is possible* were the first words I read on the flyer. Was it? After ten years of slavery to food and weight and self-hate and obsession about my appearance, this sounded unfathomable. But wonderful. Complete freedom from food – the ability to live life without obsessing over weight or appearance. *Can a woman even live like that?* I wondered.

After a decade of restricting, binging, purging, taking diet pills, smoking, and compulsively working out, I was finally defeated and tired. I knew that I could no longer maintain the lifestyle, habits, and rules to which I had become accustomed. More importantly, I finally didn't want to anymore. So I signed up for the program. I didn't necessarily think I had an eating disorder, and hadn't put a name to my behaviours. I just thought I had 'strange eating habits'. But I was fed up with the way I was living my life, believed that God had more for me, and wanted to know what freedom felt like.

Sitting at the first night of the New ID program, I listened to the instructor explain the types of eating disorders. When she was through covering anorexia, bulimia and binge-eating, I was dumbfounded. *What? You don't have to starve yourself or throw up to have an eating disorder?* I hadn't developed a cookie-cutter condition; you couldn't label it, and you couldn't even recognise it from the outside. I had maintained a normal weight throughout my entire battle. Although you couldn't spot my struggle in a crowd, it was real. And the illness, addiction and desperate attempt to cope and control were the same.

I finally realised I had a problem, and I wanted to fix it. But it wasn't going to be easy. Going through my old journals, I wondered where the whole problem had started. Mean things people had said, a traumatic experience in college – recovery brought much more with it than the box of Coco Pops I'd eaten the night before. Recovery brought up some very real, painful issues that I would rather not have dealt with, but had to. And suddenly I realised I couldn't do this on my own. I was going to need God, and a psychologist.

The psychologist had a catchphrase: 'Let's be fair.' She was right; I was being too hard on myself, expecting perfection, and not giving myself credit for my small victories in recovery and personal growth. I hadn't realised how much my eating disorder had been a crutch. At the first sign of an uncomfortable emotion or thought, I would begin obsessing about what I'd eaten that day, what I was going to eat, when I was going to work out – something, anything that was in my control. I had to learn again how to experience the highs and lows in my own life.

The psychiatrist was helpful for giving me an insight into how my mind was working, but in the meantime God also gave me a verse that was important in my recovery process: Galatians 5:1 *(see below)*. While Paul was not speaking about mental health or eating disorders here, the idea of embracing freedom from my eating disorder and not allowing the yoke of it to take hold of my life was very powerful in my recovery. True freedom would only be found through Christ because I could not truly know my identity or worth without looking to Christ for the answers. After so many years looking to the world for answers, I had misplaced my identity and worth. Great peace came with the idea of receiving grace because of what Jesus did for me without it being tied to my performance.

When I surrendered my eating disorder to God, I realised that I was actually safest when I was in a posture of vulnerability and openness, not rigidity and control. We cannot surrender halfway when it comes to our relationship with God – we are either holding the reins or letting them go. There is no true freedom without surrender. While it feels scary and paradoxical, you will be safest when you surrender to God and open yourself to receiving grace.[1]

---

1   Adapted from blog: https://joyfulandexpectant.wordpress.com/my-story/ Reproduced with permission.

For freedom Christ has set us free; stand firm therefore, and do not submit again to a yoke of slavery. (Gal. 5:1, ESV)

೦ⴰ⥬ⴰ೦

The tyrant

One of the greatest things about living in a democracy is the sense of being in charge of your own destiny. You can control who gets into power, or even run for office yourself. You can control where you want to live, what kind of job you do, who you marry. You can say what you want, read what you want, believe what you want, make mistakes and make amends – even rip up the whole life you've made and start over with new goals.

Now imagine living in a regime ruled by a tyrant. The tyrant tells you what is right and wrong, good and bad. The tyrant makes you live within strict rules and jealously relegates your relationships. The tyrant watches you so closely that you are afraid to even utter a question aloud about the regime; if you fall out of favour, your whole way of life could be destroyed, and even though you now live with impossible goals and demands, it's the only way you know how to live. The tyrant has complete control over every aspect of your life, and no matter how carefully you follow the laws, you are being constantly condemned for your failures.

Now imagine that you ARE the tyrant. You are also the subject. To have complete control over your life, you must cede *all* freedom to your own self-imposed rules. You don't want anyone to threaten or overthrow the tyrant, because that would threaten your very being. Even though your brain can see how illogical it is, in your core you would rather die than be free.

There are countless reasons why people have an unhealthy relationship with food. We live in a civilisation addicted to bingeing on unhealthy foods, then veering to starvation diets before special occasions; we idolize super-thin or super-fit people even while the majority of the population is overweight; we spend too much time online, where girls are bullied and where eating disorders and self-harm can become fetishized; we have an overly honed sense of what is cool or stylish, and prize those above what is substantial and intellectual.

'Save yourself – just a little bit.'

But above all, the problem that people with anorexia, bulimia, binge-eating disorders, and all of us along that spectrum have in common is that *we want to be God*. We all have that little tyrannical voice inside, whispering *Do what feels right to you. Create your own world. Save yourself – just a little bit.* If you think you're nothing like an anorexic, ask yourself what things you're discontented with in your life, and what you could do to change them. If you just thought 'I could start online dating' or 'Maybe if I set up an extra savings account,' you're thinking of ways that you could control your life. Now, obviously we are not meant to be passive people; God tells us to work hard, for example, while trusting Him to provide for our needs. But very often we get things the wrong way round. We think 'What can I do?' first, and it only occurs to us far down the line to 'bring all our requests before

God, with thanksgiving'.[2] We all have to fight back against the tyrant, bringing our whole spiritual armour into the fray. An advanced eating disorder – whether in the woman furious at herself for consuming more than three hundred calories in one day, or the woman who eats three hundred calories just to console herself for what she sees in the mirror – shows us plainly what it looks like when the tyrant inside gains control over someone's life.

A word to the majority of women, who don't have a medically-defined eating disorder: if you're wondering how anyone loses control of her eating habits, bear in mind that most of us can't claim much moral high ground here. We have all criticised an actress on TV for her looks. We have all indulged in lazy eating, comfort eating, idolization of food, gluttony.[3] We have laughed at our weaknesses and our lack of fitness. We have made or ordered way too much food and wasted half of it. We need to acknowledge sin in our relationship with food, and to repent of it. Over-eating is one of the sins taken least seriously in our churches, even though it severely curtails our health and adds to the terrible food shortages around the world. I am speaking to no one here so much as to myself. And even though most of us don't have medically recognised disorders, most of us also struggle with the attitudes and anxieties that create them.

---

2   Phil. 4:6, my summary.

3   'Gluttony' usually refers to excessive eating in public, for example the all-you-can-eat buffet! Over-eating out of pain, as a form of self-medication, is usually done in private as it can trigger feelings of shame.

Who do you believe?

Eating disorders are serious mental illnesses and there are genetic, biological, societal and environmental factors at play. However, they are often triggered by four motivations: **coping** with the ups and downs of life, **controlling** what you can when life feels unstable,

our inner tyrant has to bend the knee to this King – every single day.

conforming to society's or your own unrealistic standards, and **comforting** yourself with food (more often associated with bingeing or bulimia). I know zero women who do not contend with these issues. I know zero humans who do not contend with these issues! Eating disorders often start with these negative emotions and spiral into an addiction.

Christie described spending hours in the mirror, staring with loathing at her body's every blemish. A high percentage of women and girls with eating disorders also self-harm or attempt suicide. Because we as women can be fixated on self-hatred, it feels oddly tender looking at the Bible's hard command 'to die to self': 'I have been crucified with Christ. It is no longer I who live, but Christ who lives in me. And the life I now live in the flesh I live by faith in the Son of God, who loved me and gave himself for me.'[4] God is so good to us! He knows that we long to discard our 'old selves', to depose our tyrants – even if that is unthinkable. He knows that our longing to live abundantly can only be fulfilled when that tyrant is dead (Rom. 5-8). He offers us His own Son's

---

4   Galatians 2:20, ESV.

death and His own Son's resurrection. But our inner tyrant has to bend the knee to this King – every single day. There is no other way to live in His kingdom of freedom. This means submission to His ways, and to His view of us as His subject.

Living as His loyal subject means that we don't give room for our old tyrant's voice hissing in our ear, *You are not good enough*. Listening to that voice is nothing but a betrayal of the One who died for us. Instead look at how Jesus responded to the devil during His temptation in the wilderness. For every insidious offer the devil makes – offering Jesus an easy way out, a shortcut around the crucifixion, control of all the world's kingdoms under only Satan's headship – Jesus counters his false promises with the truth of God's Word. And even when Satan tries to twist Scripture to fit his own purposes (I'm pretty sure I've done this!) Jesus calls him out on it. He knows the Bible. He knows what His Father was really saying, even when Satan takes it out of context. As with so many of the things we need to overcome, knowing Scripture is absolute key. Read it in huge chunks to get context like Rosaria Butterfield. Internalise it like Elisabeth Elliot. Allow the 'two-edged' sword to surgically explore your heart and root out sin and rot.

Remember that, like the devil, your inner tyrant is NOT trustworthy. The promises of the Bible ARE trustworthy. God has proven Himself over and over again. As 1 John 3:20 (ESV) says, 'for whenever our heart condemns us, God is greater than our heart, and he knows everything'. Don't listen to your conscience if it condemns you over your own self-imposed rules! Bring any sense of guilt or condemnation to

Christ, confess what you must and ask Him to cleanse and comfort you. Beyond that, any sense of condemnation is the voice of the Accuser. Give it no space in your head or heart.

Long ago, I wrote a column for a Christian teen magazine. The column was called *Don't Think It, Pray It*, and it was about how to 'pray constantly' – about little things and big, talking to God about all worries as you would to a friend, rather than turning them over and over in your mind. Praying constantly is the only way to counter a constant worry or temptation. Train yourself to pray every time you hear that voice. Deflect its nagging away from your heart, which is not qualified to deal with it, and to God's ear instead. 'The tyrant is telling me I'm not good enough today,' tell the Lord. 'Is that true?' And hear Him say, 'No, my child. You are accepted in the Beloved.'

One of the *downsides* about living in a democracy is the importance it places on the individual. Of course individuals are important – there is no society without them! – but our civilisation encourages us to make demigods of ourselves. 'You're special.' 'You deserve it.' 'We're all winners.' 'Don't let anything stand in your way.' 'You can be anything.' It's not very conducive to dying to self, is it? Mirrors are good things. They help us do our mascara without poking ourselves in the eye. They point out that stain we forgot was on our T-shirt. They remind us it's time to get our fringe cut. But so often what we see in the mirror becomes our primary focus, our definition of ourselves. Not who we are in Christ, but who we look like to others.

If you're struggling with an eating disorder, you might need to spend less time with mirrors for a while. You might need to resist examining your bones, or your dimples. Instead know who you are in Christ – and look at Him. Make up a list of verses that remind you of who He is, what He's like, and what He's done for you.

It is important to find outside help, too. Christie says:

> The three things critical for recovery are faith/scripture to maintain a right relationship with God, community and accountability to establish a right relationship with others, and clinical experts to help develop a right relationship with self.

A fist or a kiss

Emma Scrivener reached a place of total isolation and physical and emotional deterioration through anorexia. She wrote a book about her experience called *A New Name*: I cannot recommend it highly enough for anyone who has felt desperation through an eating disorder or a need to control their life. Here she describes her moment of surrender after realising she had cut herself off from the support even of her family.

> In trying to save myself, I had destroyed everything I had said I loved. I had come to the end of myself: I knew nothing. ...Morality – my rules – seemed to offer redemption, but choked me instead. The rituals that promised salvation were iron-forged manacles that took me to hell.
>
> I'd made my home in the darkness. I'd forgotten everything but myself. When the light came, I shrank from it, but, without God, I had no self to speak of.
>
> This was it: the end. There was nowhere left to go.
>
> In desperation, I cried out to the God I'd fought so hard to escape.

'Lord,' I said, 'I'm done. I give up. I've been running and running, and I'm tired. I'm not in control. I want to be, and I've tried to be – my whole life. It doesn't work. I can't do it any more. If you'll have it, take what's left and do with it whatever you want.

...In Romans 2 there's a verse that I've never understood. It says this: 'God's kindness leads you toward repentance' (2:4).

My version of repentance had no room for kindness. Instead, it was about fear, pride and self-will. My version said, 'Pull yourself together. Try harder, do more, make it better. Fix your own mistakes – or face the consequences.'

But real repentance looks very different. It's the product of God's kindness, undeserved and poured out without limit. As I stood before the Lord, I expected a fist. He gave me a kiss. What finally floored me was grace. This is what brought me to my knees.[5]

Can I bear fruit?

If you are struggling with an eating disorder, can you still be fruitful in God's kingdom? **Yes.** There is unlikely to be a 'quick fix' for this fight. It may require outside help from a counsellor, a psychiatrist, a doctor, or medication. It may even be a lifelong 'thorn in the flesh'.[6] But if you let God fight for you – not fighting by yourself, not controlling the battle by

---

5   Scrivener, Emma, *A New Name: Grace and Healing for Anorexia* (London: IVP, 2012), chapter 8, 'Revelation', heading 'Real Repentance'. Emma also blogs at emmascrivener.net

6   In 2 Corinthians 12:7-10 Paul speaks about his 'thorn in the flesh', a physical ailment (thought to be an eye ailment) which constantly niggled him. Though he asked God three times to heal him, he eventually realised that God allowed this difficulty to remain in order

yourself – you will bear the fruit of the Spirit, and you will be a beacon of proof to the world that Christ overcomes in us. That new life is possible. That the tyrants of devil and self are truly dead. You have a unique opportunity to show that you are not defined by what you eat or what you weigh, and you will show the strength and courage and joy that could only come from the Creator. You can show that wonderful gift, acceptance – acceptance by the Father, and your own acceptance of who you are in Christ.

The tyrant is dead. Long live the King.

Questions

1. What areas of your life do you feel are outside of your control, and what do you do to achieve certain outcomes or feel more secure in those areas?

2. How do you think God sees you? When you consider repentance, do you expect Him to respond to you with a fist or a kiss?

3. What would change in your life if you died wholly to self, and lived wholly in Christ? Does that sound like a painful transformation, a freeing one, or both?

Turn your eyes upon Jesus
Look full in his wonderful face
And the things of earth will grow strangely dim
In the light of his glory and grace.
—Helen Howarth Lemmel

---

to keep Paul both dependent on Him and humble even as he soared to new spiritual heights.

7 Illness

Susannah Spurgeon

Susannah did not have a particularly promising childhood or youth in spiritual terms. Her parents went occasionally to a Baptist congregation, with Susie attending somewhat more regularly with her evangelical cousins. Aged about twenty, Susie made a profession of faith after a challenging sermon, but the gospel did not seem at that point to penetrate deep into her heart. She did not make a rigorous habit of Bible-reading or prayer, and her faith remained immature and even doubtful. She still went to church only when her cousins took her along – and she was unimpressed with a forceful but unpolished nineteen-year-old preacher who was causing a sensation in their church.

She found the young, heavyset, rustic Mr Spurgeon uncouth, and listened more intently to his country accent than his passionate exposition of God's love. The congregation, however, were electrified. Mr Spurgeon was immediately called to the church as their minister, and as Susie's cousins were some of his greatest supporters, they often met together over the tea or dinner table. Mr Spurgeon's love of God was irresistible, and before long Susie was confiding in him her doubts and discouragements about her faith. A love that sparked over discussions of the Bible and *Pilgrim's Progress* burst into flame one morning at London's Crystal Palace when Charles asked Susie, 'Do you ever pray for your future husband?' It was clear who he had in mind, and the blushing young couple began their courtship wandering together over the pleasure grounds of the Exhibition.

During their engagement, Susie was still vying to be first in her fiancé's heart – evidenced by a quarrel they had when Charles, distracted at a preaching engagement, allowed the large and rowdy crowd he had attracted to separate him from Susie. But Susie's mother, who had a quiet faith of her own, counselled her daughter to not only allow, but also do everything possible to encourage, Charles to always keep his service to his Lord first in his life. It was a lesson that she took to heart. As their life together developed, she not only sacrificed herself to allow Christ first place in Charles' heart; soon He was first in hers as well.

Over the next fifteen years or so, Susannah developed as a godly mother, raising her twin sons to know the Lord; a godly wife, ministering to her husband tirelessly; and a Christian, growing closer to her God through continuous Bible study, theological reading, and prayer. There was little sign of her dark clouds gathering just beyond view. The Spurgeons did face hardship – several people had been trampled and killed during one of Charles' services after some prankster yelled 'Fire!', and this seemed to trigger the episodes of depression he suffered throughout his life – but Susie's personal thorn in the flesh was yet to arrive.

About the age of thirty-five or thirty-six, Susie began to suffer long-term debilitating pain, unspecified due to its delicate nature, but probably a female complaint along the lines of endometriosis. A woman who had traversed Alpine passes on foot, such was her love of walking, was now confined to her own house. While a surgery around this time provided some relief, the rest of Susie's life would be mostly housebound, and often bedbound, by crippling, searing pain.

Her life would be hemmed in by illness – but not defined by it.

Instead, Susie's middle age was defined by her founding of, and work for, Mrs Spurgeon's Book Fund. She was grieved for the many poor pastors who could not afford any theological books at all to help them care for their small flocks, and so she invited letters from any pastors who would like a gift of books to provide him spiritual sustenance. Over the years she received thousands of these, and replied to each one, along with keeping accounts, managing stocks of books which were donated by others or which she bought herself, and writing reports on the Book Fund. Charles wrote of her 'work which has been to her fruitful in unutterable happiness'. It had,

> supplied my dear suffering companion with a happy work which has opened channels of consolation for her, imported great interest to the otherwise monotonous life of an invalid....By this means He called her away from her personal griefs, gave tone and concentration to her life, led her to continual dealings with Himself, and raised her nearer

the centre of that region where other than earthly joy and sorrows reign supreme.[1]

And though he occasionally had to encourage her to take breaks from the work when her illness or strain became too much, Susie took great enjoyment and refreshment from the Book Fund. She vividly imagined a pastor receiving the long-awaited gift of books, and falling to his knees in his threadbare study, tearfully praising God for His providence, before bringing the Word anew to his congregation. Susie could see the whole scene as if she were there, and it fed her from the solitude of her own home.

The actual thanks which she received also revived her:

> Sometimes, when I am weary and dispirited, mostly from physical causes, the Lord sends me a gracious uplifting, by the pen or the word of a friend, which causes me to take heart again, and believe that my labour has not been in vain, or without the seal of His approval. A month or two ago, during a season of heart-drought, I received [a] letter, which dropped like dew upon my soul....[2]

Her patience through opposition and illness bore the very evident 'peacable fruit of righteousness' in her character as well as her life. A few years later, when a financial contributor to the Spurgeons stopped his support as he fell on the other side of the Downgrade Controversy, Susie was able to draw on this reserve of 'fruit'. She wrote to Charles:

---

1   Rhodes, Ray Jr. *Susie: The Life and Legacy of Susannah Spurgeon, Wife of Charles H. Spurgeon* (Chicago, IL: Moody Publishers, 2018), chapter 9, 'Mrs Spurgeon's Book Fund'.

2   Ibid., chapter 13, 'A Lady of Letters'.

At once, I took the letter and spread it before the Lord, pleading, as Hezekiah did that He would 'hear and see' the words written therein; and He gave me so strong a confidence in His overruling and delivering power that, as I knelt in His presence, and told Him how completely I trusted Him on my husband's behalf, the words of petition ceased from my lips, and I absolutely *laughed out loud,* so little did I fear what man could do, and so blessedly reliant did He make me on His own love and omnipotence![3]

Charles rejoiced in his wife's confidence in the Lord, and he assured her that he shared her security. The money was soon replaced by a different source who knew nothing of the matter.

In late 1891, by what can only be described as a miracle, Susie was well enough to travel with Charles to Mentone, France, for the almost annual journey he made for his physical and mental health. There they enjoyed 'three months of perfect earthly bliss' – and there, in January 1892, Charles speedily declined and then entered the presence of his Saviour. Though distraught at her loss, Susie immediately took both her grief, and her joy on Charles' behalf, to the Lord. Later she was able to use this terrible blow to minister to others in her writing:

...the shadow of a great grief lies on the latter half of the book. ...Should I therefore have withheld its blessed story? Nay, rather, it seems fit that all should know how God comforted me in my affliction, and in His wondrous pity and compassion uplifted me, from the sorrow of my loss, into the joyful hope of eternal reunion in the land that knows no death.[4]

3   Ibid., chapter 11, 'Mentone: Happiness and a Sad Goodbye'.
4   Ibid., chapter 13, 'A Lady of Letters'.

Susannah lived until 1903, and those painful years of separation from Charles – a trial even harder than her agonising and debilitating illness – were deeply fruitful. She planted a church, raised enormous funds for a new building after a fire gutted the Metropolitan Tabernacle, and continued her work with the Book Fund. Apart from these legacies, her unfailing support of her husband enabled Charles Spurgeon to become one of the greatest and most enduring preachers in history, and her loving teaching of her two sons saw them both become ministers, one of them taking over his father's pulpit at the Tabernacle.

After her death, Charles Ray eulogized her thus:

> If greatness depends on the amount of good which ones does in the world, if it is only another name for unselfish devotion in the service of others – and surely true greatness is all this – then Mrs. C. H. Spurgeon will go down to posterity as one of the greatest women of her time.[5]

When I am weak, then I am strong. (2 Cor. 12:10b)

⟨⟨∾⟩⟩

Meet Susie: someone who understands what you're going through

Beloved Friends, it may be that, for some of you, the New Year opens in sadness and silence, without the merry crash of bells, and the welcoming cheers which celebrate its advent, and signify its joy to so many other hearts. Your trials are heavy, your comforts are few, earthly sorrows weigh

---

5   Ibid., epilogue.

you down, and hinder the glad mounting of your spirit to Heavenly places in Christ Jesus. The prospect of incessant toil and weariness oppresses you, or the restrospect of sorrow and suffering has benumbed you, and you do not feel you can heartily respond to the usual salutation of friend to friend, 'I wish you a Happy New Year,' – you would rather have done with earth, and that God gave you the wings of a dove that you might fly away and be at rest....I quite understand your feelings, I have fellowship with you in your fear and faintness of heart; but I bring afresh to you, today, the sweet and comforting assurance that your blessed Lord knows all your sorrows, sees all your sufferings, is watching over you with a Divine love and care which knows no cessation, and will, in His own good time, either revive or release you.[6]

What woman among us could fail to identify with Susie's words? We have all known the weariness, discouragement or pain that have brought us to fear and faintness of heart, an inability to enter into the joys everyone else seems to feel. Across all these years, she still writes to us as a kind and understanding friend – because Susie has truly 'been there'.

But I take comfort from the fact that Susie didn't start out as wise and patient and godly as she finished. She was not a spiritual prodigy but, on the contrary, something of a slow starter. It was through the agency of her patient and godly husband that Susie truly started out on the 'narrow path', and through the power of the Holy Spirit that she was sustained even when she was journeying alone. It gives me hope that God may yet grow the godly, nurturing character in me that

6   Ibid., chapter 13, 'A Lady of Letters'.

I so admire in my older Christian friends! And it warns me that God so often uses suffering to do so. Susie's words are to me both an encouragement and a loving reproof: 'If we would trust Him for the keeping, as we do for the saving, our lives would be far holier and happier than they are.'[7]

The Word that sustains

As in so many of these chapters, the first thing to notice about Susie's experience of overcoming is that she did so by the power of the Word; and that power was available to her because she so fully abided in Scripture, reading it ravenously and memorising it to be ready in her moment of need.

Isaiah 61 promises a Saviour who is able to give to His servants 'the garment of praise instead of a faint spirit (in some translations, a spirit of despair or heaviness)'. We need this promise because there are times of our life to which the *natural* reaction would be despair. It can only be a work of the Lord to turn our darkest moments into an opportunity to praise Him instead! This is beautifully illustrated by a lesson Susie drew from her garden:

> As she gathered the roses, she caught a bloom that was falling to the ground. She noticed that it was besprinkled with water. She then perceived that 'shake of the rose' had brought forth water from its 'inmost recesses'. The reservoir of water, contained within all of Susannah's roses, had strengthened them 'against the heat of the day' and refreshed them with

---

7   Ibid.

water from within. She applied her discovery to Christians struggling under the 'heat and burden of the day'.[8]

Like Susie, and her roses, do you have 'reservoirs' of the Word and remembrances of the Lord's hand in your life that may refresh you in times of suffering?

The praise that sustains

When we think of invalids, we picture someone who is weak, fearful, lonely, bitter. While Susie no doubt had to fight these feelings, she shows no evidence of living in them. She had seen God's provision so greatly in her life, and had internalised so much of His Word, that she continued to praise Him. She praised Him even when she could barely speak, much less write:

> Sometimes I have prayed, 'Do, dear Lord, enable me to write, if only a brief paragraph, just to tell of all Thy mercy and loving-kindness to me; let me praise Thee from out of the depths: into which Thou didst bring me!...But I found that His will for me was that I should be silent; He locked up thoughts and words, restrained all mental activity, and brought me so low that a sense of absolute powerlessness bound both body and spirit.[9]

In her 'absolute powerlessness', Susie found the power of the Lord. In her inability to praise Him aloud, she was still full of the will to praise Him from the depths of her heart. In her 'restrained mental activity', she rested completely in her Saviour. In this submission to His will, she found a contentment that

---

8   Ibid., epilogue.
9   Ibid., chapter 15, 'Seeing the King and His Glory'.

many of us who are fit in mind and body pass over as we focus on all the bustle, accomplishments and acquisitions of life! Susie could instead turn her gaze fully on the beauty of the Lord.

None of us has an excuse to be ineffective in the Lord's kingdom.

Part of the reason behind Susie's thankfulness was that she had trained herself to see the Lord's hand in absolutely everything – in her roses, in creation, in provision, in her pain itself. She knew there was nothing that was not under His care and direction, and she could not but praise Him for all that she saw, as well as the sensation of His sweet company in her sickroom.

The work that sustains

None of us has an excuse to be ineffective in the Lord's kingdom. Each of us has spiritual gifts, and it is a sin not to use them for God's glory. In lovingly and thankfully fulfilling His purposes for us, we find our greatest joy and usefulness. Susie's work for the Book Fund was not only God's 'manna' for pastors suffering in poverty, but also His 'manna' for Susie's desert of suffering. How easy it is to become depressed and frustrated when we are without purpose! Yet the work we can do for God's kingdom is endless. Writing an encouraging email, offering (as a health-challenged friend of mine recently did) to be a listening ear to anyone who needs to talk, witnessing to non-Christian friends about God's goodness even through hardship, or supporting the Lord's work financially, even in small ways, are things most of us could do.

And let us not forget that the effectual, fervent prayer of a righteous man (or woman!) avails much[10] – there is no such thing as 'just' prayer. Prayer is a powerful weapon which each one of us can wield and by which each one of us can make an enormous, palpable difference in people's lives and in the world. Prayer only feels like a small thing if we forget that all the power and provision is in God's hands, not our own. The phrase 'prayer warrior' is one which has been overused; but let's think a moment about the word *warrior*, remembering that 'we do not wrestle against flesh and blood, but against the rulers, against the authorities, against the cosmic powers over this present darkness, against the spiritual forces of evil in the heavenly places' (Eph. 6:12, ESV). It is a real battle, and you are a real warrior – even if you are too weak to move!

> *It is a real battle, and you are a real warrior – even if you are too weak to move!*

Two things strike me about Susie's work. First, it was focused on others. Too often our prayer lives become all about ourselves and our needs; we may even start out praying, but lose focus and veer into anxiety and self-pity! But Susie knew there was great need in the Church and that her illness was also an opportunity to enter a new sphere of ministry. Second, her motivation (thankfulness and Christ-centredness) came before the result (the Book Fund). Serving God out of

> *Serving God out of duty... leads to work that is prayerless and burdensome.*

---

10   James 5:16, KJV.

duty, or to bring credit to ourselves, or to occupy ourselves, leads to work that is prayerless and burdensome. Susie's work was so Christ-focused that it benefited her as much as the pastors she served.

> 'I found that to "do the next thing" was earnestly to set to work at the Book Fund' [Susie wrote]. Money was still flowing into the Fund and she confidently declared, 'I fully believed that God constrained me to the service, and strengthened me for it, in order to keep heart and mind from dwelling too constantly upon my loneliness and grief.' She credited God for using the Fund for her benefit, saying, 'Many a trial has been lightened by the uplifting of its sweet ministry; and many a dark day has been made bright at eventide by the encouragement granted to my loving efforts.' She described the Fund as serving her 'in the deepest sorrow my life can ever know,' pointing to 'the consoling power of active service for the Lord and His poor servants.'[11]

Following in Christ's footsteps

In Colossians 1:24 (ESV), Paul startlingly writes that 'in my flesh I am filling up what is lacking in Christ's afflictions.' We know that Christ, suffering under the weight of sin as well as the physical agony of crucifixion, was afflicted more than any other person, so what does this verse mean?

Peter Leithart explains it thus:

He's confident that his trials benefit the Church because he's convinced they are not *his* sufferings. Paul labors, is beaten times beyond number, continually faces death; he is lashed,

---

11   *Susie,* chapter 12, 'With Christ, Which Is Far Better'.

shipwrecked, in danger from Jews and Gentiles, threatened in city and country, hungry, thirsty, cold. Paul is the subject of all these miseries, but they aren't his own. They are the 'afflictions of Christ,' though they occur in Paul's own flesh.[12]

In our suffering, do we complain and worry and grow bitter, or do we 'fill up the afflictions of Christ' by offering up patient and praise-filled suffering as a sacrifice to Him? Do we testify to the world of our loving trust in our Saviour, and therefore point them back to *His* sufferings on their behalf?

If this prospect feels to you somewhat daunting, as it does to me, take heart from Susie's encouragement.

A year after Charles' death, she wrote: 'Dear fellow-Christian, do not faint or fear when the blessed Husbandman cuts, and grafts, and wounds thee!' She encouraged her readers to not be as much concerned about the pain the grafting causes but more that fruit should come through suffering. She was convinced that God does not forget His people but 'watches with loving scrutiny every indication of developing fruit-buds' and that 'great will be His joy, when, in full strength and beauty, thou shalt glorify Him by thy abundant fruitfulness.' She declared, 'Yet how good God has been to me! He has upheld me through days of darkness, and seasons of sorrow, of which none knew but Himself and my own soul.'[13]

Can I still bear fruit?

It is clear from Susie's example that seasons of illness and weakness can be times when we bear the *most* fruit, and know

---

12   www.firstthings.com blog post, 3/9/18.

13   *Susie,* chapter 8, 'The Great Sufferer'.

the Lord's tenderest presence. His strength is made perfect in our weakness. In fact, this may be the time in our lives when we can give Him the most glory.

> When the storms come, and our trees of delight are bare and leafless, when He strips us of the comforts to which His love has accustomed us – or more painful still, – when He leaves us alone in the world, to mourn the absence of the chief desire of our heart; –to sing to Him *then,* to bless and praise and laud His dear name *then,* this is the work of His free grace only.[14]

Questions

1. What is a time that you have endured illness or another trial that, looking back, you can see the Lord used to bring you closer to Himself or make you more useful in His Kingdom?

2. When life gets hard, do you turn inward and focus on your suffering, or do you turn to serving God? What are some practical steps you could take to turn your attention on others' needs when you are feeling weak or low yourself?

3. What are some things that you need to 'lay before the Lord', as Susie did her discouraging letter, and ask Him to strengthen your trust that He will provide?

> *When peace like a river attendeth my way,*
> *When sorrows like sea-billows roll;*
> *Whatever my lot, thou hast taught me to say*
> *'It is well, it is well with my soul.'*
> —Horatio Spafford

---

14 Ibid., epilogue.

8 False Beliefs

Doreen Virtue

A public transformation

I was sitting in a creche café when another mum friend, who happened to be an interfaith minister, asked me if I had heard of Doreen Virtue. I had not.

'She's probably the biggest name in the New Age community,' my friend told me. 'It's a bit more airy-fairy than the mindfulness I take part in, but I know other people who follow her. She's especially famous for writing angel cards – how you can get angels to bring you peace or intervene in your life.'

'Oh right,' I said, wondering how to explain about the biblical purpose of angels. But that wasn't what my friend was getting at.

'Well, a year or two ago, Doreen Virtue converted to Christianity – really publicly. She denounced all her old works and says they're of the devil. A lot of New Age people have felt very upset and angry. What do Christians think about someone like that? I imagine you wouldn't accept her either

– it could be just a publicity stunt, to sell Christian books instead. How do you ever trust someone who was so vocal for another religion?'

Of course, I immediately googled Doreen Virtue. Dozens of books came up, all esoteric, with titles like *Angel Numbers, Chakra Learning,* and *Archangels & Ascended Masters.* I went further, to Doreen's website, and found there a complete testimony of how she had only recently discovered the falsehood and danger of the New Age, that Jesus was the only true way to salvation, and that she wanted to discourage anyone from buying her old work. Her message was biblical and heartfelt. Case closed, as far as I was concerned.

'Christians have no difficulty with this,' I told my friend. 'We all have experienced how completely Christ changes us, so we actually expect to see it happen in others. In fact, when someone so visible becomes a Christian, we think of it as something of a victory, and welcome them into the family.'

I have since learned that that is not quite true – that there are Christians who are distrustful of new converts, and spend considerable time examining their lives for any inconsistencies, without investing time or patience or personal discipleship. I think we can learn both from Doreen's example of true life in Jesus, and from the example of those who have persecuted her as a new Christian.

Doreen now spends her time warning people against the dangers of the New Age and pointing them to the one true Way to peace. What follows is a condensed version of her story, which you can explore more fully at doreenvirtue.com.

In Her Own Words

I grew up in a Christian Scientist/universalist church, and saw visions from early childhood. I became a counsellor as a grown-up, and after an experience with New Age beliefs at a conference, I started working New Age doctrine into my counselling service. My clients found me perceptive and comforting, and before long I was writing books for the religious/inspirational publisher Hay House. My career really took off once I started writing about angels and the effect they could have on people's lives, and I became Hay House's bestselling author, with over fifty products.

I was channelling people's fortunes and using tarot cards, but I was frightened of the occult and threw out the 'scary' cards. Despite being known for writing about angels, I wouldn't study fallen angels. I wouldn't watch horror movies or even pick up *Harry Potter!* On the outside I was thriving – I lived on a 40-acre property in Hawaii with my husband Michael and my own animal rescue – but I lived in fear. And while I was teaching people what to believe and how to live their lives, I was searching for deeper and deeper secret wisdom. I felt that someone had hidden the real truth from me. The New Age is about trying to predict and control the future, but the devil can give only the illusion of control.

In 2015 I was working on a pack of Jesus cards: inspirational thoughts about Jesus that people could lean on in their lives for comfort without delving too much into the Bible or its demands! Although I didn't really know Jesus, I had a healthy respect for him and knew I had to be careful, so I was going to put only scriptural quotations on the cards. I was familiar with the KJV Bible from childhood, and I got a version with red letters so I could find his words more easily.

What I found was Mark 8:38, and my life changed right there. 'If anyone is ashamed of me and my message in these adulterous and sinful days, the Son of Man will be ashamed of that person when he returns in the glory of his father, with the holy angels.' I had grown up thinking that Jesus was love, and that meant that anything goes. Everyone was going to heaven; we don't judge; we love everyone equally. And God does love everyone, but sin creates a wedge between them and him. When I read all the restrictions and boundaries Jesus taught, I was gobsmacked!

In 2016 Michael and I started attending a Pentecostal church, but I was trying to walk in both worlds. I said the sinners' prayer and meant it; I took communion; but I was still going home to tarot cards, psychic readings and channelling books! I learned the hard way that oil and water don't mix. You can't keep sinning and come to the Lord. You can't serve two masters.

I left that church for superficial reasons and went to an Episcopal church. They were super nice, and they confronted me about my New Age beliefs – but they were subtle. Subtlety doesn't work on someone whose eyes are blinded by the devil. If you know someone who's deceived by the New Age, you have to speak up. I needed someone to sit me down and tell me the gospel of Jesus. No one was courageous enough. I don't place the responsibility for my wandering on them; I knew I should be reading the whole Bible, and I was putting it off. But I wish I had had more guidance from Christians.

In January 2017, I had a life-changing vision of Jesus. At first I was certain I had seen the Lord, but that raises some important questions, and even now I am not sure whether it was truly a vision from God or a demon masquerading as

Jesus. But the vision wasn't what saved me anyway – it just got my attention. It was reading Deuteronomy 18:10-12 later in 2017 that convicted me of my sins and caused me to repent and ask Jesus to be my Lord and Saviour. I read that the fortune-telling, divination, and mediumship I'd been doing made me an abomination to God. This broke me! Up until then, I really thought I was 'doing God's work' because my readings seemed to bring people comfort.

I had an epiphany that the Bible and Jesus were true. I suddenly understood what it meant that he died for our sins. I dropped to my knees in sorrow, and deeply repented. I kept saying to God, 'I'm sorry! I didn't know!' I realised how much of my life was a mess because I'd relied upon 'angels' (which I now realise were demons in disguise), instead of studying the Bible and trusting in God. All I know is that *something* happened that day on January 7, 2017, and the result was that I was pointed to read the entire Bible, which resulted in my salvation that same year.

In the New Age, 'sin' doesn't exist, and saying I was a 'sinner' would be equivalent to saying I was a bad person. Indeed, the devil does bring about self-loathing – but only for the purposes of condemnation, not renewal. He wants people to be seekers on his terms, away from the Bible. He only gives misery – not 'sorrowing after a godly sort',[1] which leads to repentance and receiving God's grace. Having peace with God is not about self-love or affirmation or acceptance. When we focus on glorifying God, and put Jesus on the throne instead of ourselves, then our self-loathing is gone. We don't need self-love, we need God-love.

---

1   2 Corinthians 7:9, KJV.

I was one of those people who believed there are many paths to God, and if you're a good person, you go to heaven. But every one of us breaks the commandments every day – and you have to confess before God every day. It's not a question of whether you sin, it's what you do about it! I can't describe what a huge miracle it is for me to believe in sin, the devil and hell. In the New Age, we wouldn't sing the line in *Amazing Grace,* 'to save a wretch like me' – because saying you were a wretch was not affirming! Now I know I was a wretch.

Immediately upon repenting, I knew I had to leave the New Age, and people were not going to like that. But I was called to follow Galatians 1:10 – 'For am I now seeking the approval of man, or of God? Or am I trying to please man? If I were still trying to please man, I would not be a servant of Christ.' I learned to be not a people-pleaser, but a God-pleaser.

Now, my sanctification process has been like someone from a foreign land learning a new language and culture! It's been an onion-peeling process, figuring out from the Bible and Holy Spirit how I need to change to live as a real Christian. I've done everything I can think of to recall all my old New Age products and discourage people from buying them, but I haven't been able to stop people selling them on. I'm doing my best to get 25 years of material either out of print, getting my name removed from the tarot cards, or replaced by Christian products. It's been a very public sanctification process. I'm spending hours each day in the Bible and praying constantly, and I've even led a Bible study online, even though I was still quite a new Christian.

In the meantime, I've stopped profiting from my old publications. Even though Hay House has not yet taken everything out of print, all of the proceeds go to charity or to pay off my tax bill. I relate to the slave girl in Acts 16, whose owners were furious when her fortune-telling spirit was cast out. I was also a cash cow for the publishers and conventions. When my channelling abilities were cast out by Jesus, I was glad – I didn't want them anymore!

Having been involved in the spirit world for 58 years, it was not a surprise to find that 'our battle is not against flesh and blood'. After my conversion, there was a time of spiritual warfare. I felt oppressed by insomnia, confusion and exhaustion. On one occasion I saw a terrifying vision of a man at the foot of my bed, holding a bazooka, and I cried out, calling on the name of Jesus. I started reading spiritual warfare books, but only one thing worked for me getting rid of this demonic oppression – focusing on Isaiah 61, in the KJV. *'The spirit of the Lord God is upon me, for the Lord has anointed me. [I have come to give] beauty for ashes...the garment of praise for the spirit of heaviness.'* The kryptonite for demons is to thank and praise and adore God. Every time I felt that unwanted heaviness and confusion, I would start to thank and praise and adore God. There is no room for demonic presence where God is being worshipped.

Of course, I had more to repent of than my involvement in the New Age. Some people have raised questions about my unusual name, thinking that it's just a pseudonym. In fact, Doreen was my given name at birth, and Virtue was my first husband's last name, so Doreen Virtue was my legal name for many years. New Age marriages are similar to Hollywood marriages: short, contentious, and built on egos and substance abuse. I fell for the New Age lies that you can find your soulmate twin flame, a person who will completely understand you and there would be no conflict. So every time in these New Age marriages that we had conflict in relationships, we thought that meant we were with the wrong person, so we would split up and go looking for our soulmate again. I know that sounds insane, and it is because the New Age is insanely delusional. That's why I must expose the New Age, because it causes so much damage.

I realise this puts a giant scarlet A on my chest. I was like the woman at the well when Jesus saved me. Sometimes those who sin the most, like me, are the most grateful for salvation and God's mercy. The woman at the well was one of the first evangelizers, telling everybody in the Samaritan community that Jesus was the Messiah. Amazing grace that saved a wretch like me!

And, believe me, I have repented and repented to God for my sin of divorce. I've also apologized to my sons many times for how they were hurt. But instead of wallowing in self-flagellation, I am choosing to remain public and expose the sins of the New Age so that others don't fall into the traps that I was in for so long.

Lots of people have gotten mad about me leaving the New Age and stopped buying my products – and it actually helps. I don't want anyone buying my old books or cards! When someone writes an angry blog about me leaving the New Age, two good things happen. One is that people who are offended stop buying my stuff. The other is that people who are intrigued by Jesus come and seek me out. I'm easy to get hold of and I'm happy to answer people's questions and pray with them. Genesis 50:20 says 'you meant evil against me, but God meant it for good'.

I've been able to pray for my enemies. This is a complete miracle for someone who was so scared of people's opinions. Some Christians are very forgiving and have welcomed me into the fold. Others are standoffish and are reluctant to welcome this ex-heretic. I get it! But if you see wrong doctrine or hypocrisy in me, please don't throw Bible verses at me publicly instead of taking the time to engage. If you see me doing something that's not consistent with Christianity, please write to me kindly to tell me. I'll listen.

I had been a seeker my whole life – looking for a deeper and deeper secret to what made everything work, to what brought peace and security. Finally I found it. I'm not a seeker any more. In Revelation, we are shown that the scroll is open – the Lamb opened it for us. Only he was worthy! Now, instead of constantly looking for something else, I'm joyful and I know that that 'God-shaped hole' inside me has been filled.

When I am quiet and praying to the Lord, I don't look for special messages from him. God's messages to us are in the Bible. Do you want to hear a message from God out loud? Then read the Bible out loud! The devil finds ways in when we seek extrabiblical messages from God. We must seek him through the mediatorship of Christ, not anyone else. If you're unsure about certain practices, ask: Is this biblical? Is it glorifying to God?

A lot of the New Age is impatience for microwave-fast answers. I'm learning to wait on the Lord and his timing, and I urge everyone to do this. Ask God; be repentant of any sin; and trust that he hears you, as he has promised, and will answer according to his will.[2]

---

2   Doreen's testimony was adapted from Doreen Virtue, *Deceived No More: How Jesus Led Me Out of the New Age and Into His Word*, (Nashville, TN: Emanate Books, 2020) and Doreen's interview with Steven Bancarz, 16 April 2018, YouTube. Reproduced with permission.

And there is salvation in no one else, for there is no other name under heaven given among men by which we must be saved. (Acts 4:12, ESV)

⁓

What constitutes false beliefs?

Absolute truth claims are unpopular in these tolerant days. Yet Jesus tells us that He alone is the 'way, the truth, and the life. No one comes to the Father except through [Him].'[3] That remains true regardless of how unwelcome the news may be. It means that every person on earth will one day bow before this immutable fact – that Jesus is Lord, whether you believed in Him on earth or not.

False beliefs, therefore, comprise anything in which we put our trust for peace with God and eternal life. This can be New Age and the occult; any organised religion such as Islam, Buddhism, Shintoism, Hinduism, etc; and even anti-biblical ideologies such as queer theory or placing too much hope in political power to change things. It can include Christian heresies such as prosperity gospel or praying to icons. Even orthodox Jews, who do not know Jesus as Messiah, must still come to a saving faith, though we owe them a debt of love and service for their heritage as the people through whom God revealed His truth.

If you are now congratulating yourself on your biblical orthodoxy, let me go one step further and widen the net to include anything that breaks the first commandment, 'you

---

3   John 14:6.

shall have no other gods before me'. None of us can keep this commandment in our own strength. We all face temptations

the number one false religion in the West is the one we call 'being good people'

to put our security in money, in our home, in our relationships, in our accomplishments, even in our 'goodness'. Or our greatest happiness is found in sport, shopping, music, partying, or some other form of pleasure. We know in our Bible head-knowledge that all of these things are ultimately futile to complete our peace and joy and spiritual maturity, and yet we can't stop striving for them, even when we see them conflict with God's Word and His purposes for us.

You Gotta Serve Somebody

A few of you may recognise this heading as a song from Bob Dylan's Christian album *Slow Train Coming*, in which the refrain says: 'It may be the devil, or it may be the Lord, but you're gonna have to serve somebody.' In reality, most of us think we are serving ourselves. I believe the number one false religion in the West is the one we call 'being good people'. *I'm a good person, so I'll go to heaven – if there's a heaven!* This is a trap even Christians fall into when we allow our consciences to go cold; when we go through our day without any awareness of our need for Christ's grace or wisdom or strength; when we start to correct another believer without looking for the beam in our own eye.

We also fall into this trap when we give space to the Accuser, and allow him to tell us who we are. When we think we can't possibly be useful in God's kingdom because our sins or our past are insurmountable, we are equally failing in trust toward the Saviour. *We* can never be good enough, but *He* is always good enough. Self-righteousness is a terribly destructive form of pride, and I should know! Isaiah 64:6 describes all our righteousness as 'filthy rags' in God's sight. We have nothing to offer Him, and no goodness to plead before His judgment.

John Calvin described the human heart as an 'idol factory'. It's a constant fight to enjoy the good gifts of relationships, without prioritising people above God; career, without making ambition our primary focus in life; provision, without wanting more and more gadgets; peace of mind, without becoming complacent. Jesus was right when He said 'No one can serve two masters.'[4] When we put anything ahead of Him – a dynamic which, in my own experience, is constantly shifting – we are guilty of breaking the whole law, and we must plead His blood for forgiveness.

Christianity is the only religion in which we do not have to earn our way to heaven – in fact, attempting to 'earn' it ourselves just takes us further away from the complete reliance on God in which our peace lies.

Designer thoughts

This title comes from one of my favourite preachers, Messianic (Jesus-believing) rabbi Cosmo Panzetta. In this sermon[5] he talks about Jesus' temptation in the wilderness, and how Satan

---

4   Matthew 6:24.

5   https://www.youtube.com/watch?v=YjUYYv0LqIU, House of New Beginnings, 7 November 2020, 'Designer Thoughts'.

[False belief:] God is strict and ready to judge us for every little thing.

planted in Him the temptations that would have appealed to Him most at that moment. He was hungry; how about a little miracle-bread? He knew He was the Son of God; why not show off a little by jumping off the roof of the Temple? He didn't want to go through a horrible death; why not take a shortcut to kingship by bowing to the prince of the earth?

In the same way, the devil prompts thoughts that hit us right where our temptations lie, and like Jesus, we must be able to rebut him with God's Word. Have you ever 'listened' to these false beliefs about God?

- God is strict and ready to judge us for every little thing. (*The Lord is merciful and gracious, slow to anger, and abounding in steadfast love* – Psalm 103:8, ESV.)

- God is going to expose us to as much suffering as possible – expect the worst. (*For I know the plans I have for you, declares the Lord, plans to prosper you and not to harm you, plans to give you hope and a future* – Jeremiah 29:11.)

- You might be going to heaven, but you've sinned too much to really be useful or peaceful right now. Maybe later, when you're doing better. (*As far as the east is from the west, so far does he remove our transgressions from us* – Psalm 103:12, ESV.)

- God blesses those who are faithful to Him, so if you're struggling with temptation or finances or illness, you're just not holy enough. Must try harder. (*Peace I leave with you; my peace I give to you. Not as the world gives do I give to you. Let not your hearts be troubled, neither let them be afraid* – John 14:27, ESV.)

• If you fail or doubt after you're saved, it's just too hard clawing your way back into God's good graces. (*Though [a good man] fall, he shall not be utterly cast down, for the Lord upholds him with His hand* – Psalm 37:24, NKJV.)

Our false beliefs can be so subtle that we don't even realise how we are drifting from the truth of God's Word. None of us has been completely faithful to God. Only Christ!

How do I help a new Christian?

If you know someone embroiled in a false belief system, first of all, don't despair. Doreen Virtue is living proof that no one is beyond God's reach – and sometimes, those who look most unattainable for His kingdom are those most vulnerable to it, as they may be 'seekers' already. But remember that there is no point asking someone to change their *practice* without changing their *heart*. Getting someone to take a Buddha off their table or a Ouija board out of their bookcase is a good first step, but it isn't the same as reliance on Jesus' sacrifice. Before they can be truly convicted of sin, and the need for repentance, they need to know the Gospel.

The Gospel is not 'The Bible says you are wrong.' The Gospel is 'Jesus is the way to heaven, the only absolute truth, and the life which lasts forever. He died as a sacrifice to pay the price for your sins, which have separated you from God. He offers you freedom from guilt and fear,

It is important to offer the Gospel as a gift, not an accusation!

peace with God, and joy in His beautiful creation. He wants people to come and serve Him as the only king, but in return He carries you through every hardship in His strength. Can I tell you some more about Jesus?'

It is important to offer the Gospel as a gift, not an accusation! As people come to know Jesus, it will be His work to bring forth repentance and change. At that point *our* work is to lovingly disciple people – not publicly judging them, as some have done to Doreen, but helping them to a greater understanding of God's Word, and raising any concerns privately and humbly, as a fellow pupil under the Master's care. There is an excellent example of this in chapter 1, where Rosaria Butterfield was able to safely open her heart to God's Word because a pastor wrote her with love and compassion instead of judgment and anger.

There can be no...dabbling in other ways to achieve security or to control the future.

In the previous section we discussed how each of us are tempted to serve masters other than Christ, and each of us must repent of our own false religion. Allow this to sink in. You are a commandment-breaker. *You have served other gods before Him.* If God could save you, then there is hope for anyone! And I say this not to point a finger, but because it's a thought that cheers me when I am worried about someone who seems hardened against God's truth. I remember that if God changed me, then no one is beyond His saving grace!

Can I bear fruit as a convert from another religion?

Yes. And the only condition for you is the same as for any new believer: you must belong to Christ alone – as the wedding vow says, 'forsaking all others'. There can be no hedging of bets, no dabbling in other ways to achieve security or to control the future. There can be no relative truth, no 'many paths to heaven'. Any compromise undermines our trust in the Bible, our faith in Christ, and our freedom in grace. The Bible is quite clear that the things of God can have no 'communion' with the forces of darkness.

But look at what you receive in return. Let's return again to one of the sweetest passages of scripture, Matthew 11:28-30 (ESV), 'Come to me, all who labor and are heavy laden, and I will give you rest. Take my yoke upon you, and learn from me, for I am gentle and lowly in heart, and you will find rest for your souls. For my yoke is easy, and my burden is light.' (If you don't already know this aria in Handel's *Messiah*, feel free to go and listen to it now – it will never leave you!) There is a delightful lightness that comes after repentance. A famous scene from John Bunyan's *Pilgrim's Progress* illustrates this beautifully.

> Up this way, therefore, did burdened CHRISTIAN run; but not without great difficulty, because of the load [of sin] on his back.
>
> He ran thus till he came at a place somewhat ascending; and upon that place stood a Cross, and a little below, in the bottom, a sepulchre. So I saw in my dream, that just as CHRISTIAN came up to the cross, his burden loosed from

off his shoulders, and fell from off his back, and began to tumble; and so continued to do till it came to the mouth of the sepulchre, where it fell in, and I saw it no more.

Then was CHRISTIAN glad and lightsome, and said, with a merry heart,

'He hath given me rest by his sorrow,
    And life by his death.'[6]

Jesus has already taken upon Himself the weight of our sins, and in return He offers the sweet and airy weight of His glory. We know that His death was the only possible way to pay for our sins, because He Himself, in the Garden of Gethsemane, asked if there was not another way. He submitted Himself willingly to the Father's will, and as a result, 'there is one God, and there is one mediator between God and men'.[7]

Our work now is to lean fully upon Him, because He is worthy, He is good, He is true, He is faithful. And to go and tell others, with the loving invitation of the gospel, so that they too may know the one and only Way.

Questions

1. What are some false beliefs that you have carried about God in the past? What are some more verses that tell you the truth about Him?

---

6 *Pilgrim's Progress* is readily available for free online. The whole text is available here, with a dedicated page to this particular chapter: http://www.covenantofgrace.com/pilgrims_progress_loses_burden.htm

7 1 Timothy 2:5.

2. Who is someone that you secretly think is beyond hope of finding God – a celebrity, a false teacher, a hard-boiled friend or relative? Take some time to pray for them, and think about how you could make an 'invitation' of the Gospel.

3. Who or what are you most inclined to 'serve' as a false master? Ask the Lord to defeat this temptation in your heart.

No guilt in life, no fear in death:
This is the power of Christ in me.
From life's first cry to final breath,
Jesus commands my destiny.
No power of hell, no scheme of man
Can ever pluck me from his hand
Till he returns or calls me home
Here in the power of Christ I stand.
—'In Christ Alone', Stuart Townend & Keith Getty, final stanza

9 Self-Righteousness

Susanna Wesley

The youngest of twenty-five children, Susanna was born in 1669. Her father, Dr Annesley, was a Dissenting (Presbyterian) minister, but Susanna was theologically and politically precocious, and at the age of twelve she left her father's church and joined the Church of England on a matter of principle, despite the fact that her father had been badly treated by Anglicans. She was a girl always aware of duty and of rigour in her spiritual exercises.

She wrote to her famous son John Wesley, 'I will tell you what rule I observed...when I was young, and too much addicted to childish diversions, which was this – never to spend more time in mere recreation in one day than I spent in private religious devotions'.[1] This is scrupulous indeed in a child and it certainly gave Susanna a profound biblical knowledge by the time she was grown.

1   Dallimore Arnold A. *Susanna Wesley: The Mother of John & Charles Wesley* (Grand Rapids, MI: Baker Books, 1993), p. 15.

By nineteen Susanna was a woman of formidable beauty. She left her father's comfortable home to marry another former Dissenter turned Church of England clergyman, Samuel Wesley. There were problems from the start. Samuel was bad with money; while he served as a chaplain on a ship, his new wife waited for him in a boarding house. He made little provision for her, so she had to return to her father's home when it was time to deliver her first child. Samuel was always in debt, always writing to his patrons asking for relief, and currying favour with nobility and royalty through flattering poems and dedications of his theological work. Things came to a head in 1702, as mentioned in the chapter on Divorce, when Samuel abandoned his family for several months over a political disagreement with his wife.

Carrying on with her family life as best she could, Susanna put a strict schedule into place. Her routine was rigid, though not unkind, to the constantly growing brood of children, based on careful discipline at an early age which set them on a course of obedience. Susanna wrote these household structures down for the use of her own children – and I wish I had the guts to follow them myself! Spending half the night getting a child to stay in bed? 'There was no such thing allowed of in our house as sitting by a child till it fell asleep.' Dealing with tantrums? Susanna's children were given 'nothing they cried for, and instructed to speak handsomely for what they wanted'. She also set up a school for them in a dedicated room, where they were taught the basics of common education and of the Bible. Her biographer, Arthur Dallimore, argues that the focus of these lessons was somewhat moralistic:

Susanna had stated that her basic purpose was 'the saving of their souls'. Although her intentions were highly commendable, she failed during these years to mention the substitutionary nature of Christ's death and the receiving of its merits by faith. She said nothing as yet of conversion or of the assurance of salvation, but she stressed the need for regular attendance at church and at the communion, and she seems to have believed that by living a fully disciplined life and refraining from open evil they would be saved.[2]

Is it fair or demonstrable to say that Susanna never taught her children about salvation through faith in Christ alone? If her sons' experience is anything to go by, it is. John and Charles Wesley received understanding of grace through Christ like a bolt from the sky, completely transforming their view of themselves and of God. They had not learned of saving grace at their mother's knee. To her eldest son Sammy, who was studying for the ministry, she wrote:

I have such a vast inexpressible desire of your salvation, and such dreadful apprehensions of your failing in a work of so great importance; and do moreover know by experience how hard a thing it is to be a Christian, that I cannot for fear, I cannot but most earnestly press you and conjure you, over and over again, to give the most earnest heed to what you have already learned, lest at any time you let slip the remembrance of your final happiness, or forget what you have to do in order to attain it.[3]

---

2   Ibid., 61.

3   Ibid., 92.

It seems clear in this letter that Susanna was not only forgetting who 'attains' salvation for us, but was somewhat acting as Sammy's conscience, as if it were she herself who was responsible for his spiritual wellbeing and his salvation.

Through many more troubles – two house fires, the disgrace of a daughter who bore an illegitimate child, the loss of several babies, her own severe illnesses, poverty so abject that Samuel's brother wrote to chastise him for failing to provide for his own family, and finally the death of Samuel himself in 1735 – Susanna entered her final phase of life. Samuel had left her with nothing but debt, and she moved from one child's home to the next. Yet she was content and cheerful.

In 1738 John and Charles Wesley came to their thunderbolt understanding of grace through faith, a revelation to which Susanna reacted with some bewilderment; she did not make the distinction between what they felt to be *saving* faith and what she had taken as simply *assurance* of faith:

I think you are fallen into an odd way of thinking. You say that till within a few months you had no spiritual life, nor any justifying faith.

Now this is as if a man should affirm he was not alive in his infancy, because when an infant he did not know he was alive. All then that I can gather from your letter is that, till a little while ago you were not so well satisfied of your being a Christian as you are now. I heartily rejoice that you have now attained to a strong and lively hope in God's mercy through Christ. Not that I can think that you were totally without saving faith before; but it is one thing to have faith, and another thing to be sensible we have it.[4]

However, in January 1740, Susanna had something of a revelatory experience herself. Her son-in-law, the Reverend Westley Hall – who was quietly floundering in his faith, and would shortly backslide into immorality and Deism, but was still being used by the Lord – was administering Communion. Suddenly Susanna found her faith renewed. 'While my son Hall was pronouncing these words in delivering the cup to me, "The blood of our Lord Jesus Christ which was given for thee," these words struck through my heart, and I knew that God for Christ's sake had forgiven me all my sins.'

John famously leapt upon this testimony, writing to his mother that she had finally been saved from a life of works, 'a legal night of seventy years'. Susanna, rather taken aback by this dramatic proclamation, corrected him:

>...My case is rather like that of the Church of Ephesus; I have not been faithful to the talents committed to my trust, and have lost my first love...
>
>I do not, I will not, despair; for ever since my sad defection, when I was almost without hope, when I had forgotten God, yet I then found he had not forgotten me. Even then he did by his Spirit apply the merits of the great atonement to my soul, by telling me that Christ died for me.[5]

Susanna seemed to be a Christian inclined to emphasise works, almost to the extent of forgetting 'what is more needful': our

---

4   Ibid., 160.

5   Ibid., 164.

reliance upon the blood of Christ and our new life in His resurrection. She showed much evidence of salvation in her life and her writing, yet by her own admission she doubted, lost hope, and lost her first love. How wonderful that, two years before the end of her long life, God called her by name and brought her back into full assurance of her salvation through nothing but His grace, by His sacrifice.

> *...He saved us, not because of works done by us in righteousness, but according to his own mercy, by the washing of regeneration and renewal of the Holy Spirit...* (Titus 3:5, ESV)

Meet Susanna: a formidable woman

Susanna Wesley did not take an easy path. Raising a huge brood of well-behaved children, almost single-handedly in the midst of a difficult marriage, while carrying on successful ministries – she was what we might call a multitasker! Sally Davey wrote that she is often portrayed 'as some kind of frighteningly efficient home schooler with a huge family; or a super-mother in time management overdrive'.[6]

The word 'frighteningly' is informative. Most of us ordinary Christian women who struggle on in the daily slog, doing our best to nurture some sort of spiritual life while keeping our heads above water and our children's faces more or less clean, might find such a woman intimidating. Her list of childrearing principles, while certainly laudable, also sound impossible, especially if one hasn't got in 'at the

---

6   https://www.christianstudylibrary.org/article/susanna-wesley

ground floor' and implemented them since babyhood. Her spiritual ministrations sound often tender but also strident and onerous. Thankfully, lives of terrific moral energy are not what we're called to – but rather to conforming to Christ's character through His power and grace.

Just keep swimming

So much of our lives, relationships and work become simple routine. The way we speak to the kids in the morning is as automatic as our alarm clocks. We barely notice slipping that pen from the office into our pocket. We fall into the habit, without realising it, of judging or disrespecting our spouse or parents. This is especially true in times of spiritual dryness, where we show up to every church service out of habit and duty, and read a daily chapter of the Bible without prayerfulness or praise. Even our repentance is cursory – 'Forgive me for losing my temper,' without any grief over our sin or acknowledgment of the need to change, or of the Lord's ability and willingness to change us.

Outwardly respectable, even fruitful, we neglect to repent

Now, it's true that self-discipline in our spiritual lives is necessary when we're busy or stressed or just don't feel like it. But we must never allow mere duty to remain the primary motivator for bringing us before the Lord, just as we must never allow these things to be the primary method by which we change. Anyone can train themselves out of bad habits if they try hard enough. But without letting the Lord change our hearts and dress us in His righteousness, our good behaviour is nothing but putting on a costume – slipping on a 'good person' onesie over our rebellious, unwashed, neglected sin nature. Counting on our own righteousness is one of the most pernicious attitudes to drive us further from the Lord. Outwardly respectable, even fruitful, we neglect to repent of our judgmentalism, lovelessness, anxiety and impatience. Like Dory in *Finding Nemo,* we 'just keep swimming' in our current direction without allowing the Word of God to settle deep within and change us.

Taking the world on your shoulders

Living a busy Christian life without reliance on Christ is exhausting. It's not only the schedule, it's the mimicry. Christians are people who are meant to exhibit the Fruit of the

The Christian life without Christ is too hard.

Spirit – love, joy, peace, patience, goodness, gentleness, self-control. Portraying these characteristics out of a heart that is in reality constricted by overreliance on rules, fitting in with the church crowd, or storing up 'treasure in heaven' by our own accomplishments rather than through sacrifice and thanksgiving is not sustainable, and certainly not joyful. At some point cracks will show. Our inconsistency becomes obvious, we are run ragged with striving, and some people just give up. The Christian life without Christ is too hard.

we are all yoked to something

We've been looking at Jesus' invitation, 'Take my yoke upon you, and learn from me, for I am gentle and lowly in heart, and you will find rest for your souls.' It might be tempting, especially in times of tiredness, to think: *Another yoke? No thanks – I'm done with yokes.* But what Jesus knew is that we are all yoked to something. To our obligations, our goals, our families, our past. It is only if we are yoked to Jesus that our burden is light – because He carries the weight of all our sins, our regrets, our anxieties. Our job in the yoke is not to bear the weight at all, but to walk alongside Him, feeling the weight and warmth of His side, keeping in step.

How often we strive to please God by maintaining a full diary of Christian activities. But it is with Christ that God is 'well pleased'.[7] If we are in Him, God is already pleased with us. He devolves on us all of Christ's perfection, accomplishment, and sonship; all of His inheritance; all the pleasure of a parent in a delightful and obedient child. How could we ever conceive of *adding* to God's pleasure in us, when it is totally completed by His pleasure in Jesus? So we may rest, knowing that God is perfectly pleased and contented in the children which the perfect Son purchased with His blood.

Empty-handed

Once again, I have to bring another of my 'overcomers' to visit from a previous chapter! There is a passage in *The Hiding Place* where Corrie ten Boom describes her family telling a terribly fearful aunt that her death was imminent. This aunt worked tirelessly in Christian and social work, taking a great deal of pride in it and a high view of her own necessity to the work.

---

7   Matthew 3:17.

The whole family approached their Tante Jans tenderly, and presented to her a picture of a woman approaching her heavenly home with her hands full: full of good works, accomplishments, charitable donations. But at the mention of all these things, the formidable Tante Jans burst into tears. She suddenly realised that none of these

> *'Dear Jesus, I thank You that we must come with empty hands.... You have done all – all – on the Cross'*

things, for which she had spent all of her time and energy striving, had added one iota to the salvation which Christ had won on the cross. She could only come to Him on His terms, covered in His righteousness, not hers.

> But our well-meant words were useless. In front of us the proud face crumpled; Tante Jans put her hands over her eyes and began to cry. 'Empty, empty!' she choked at last through her tears. 'How can we bring anything to God? What does He care for our little tricks and trinkets?'
>
> And then as we listened in disbelief she lowered her hands and with tears still coursing down her face whispered, 'Dear Jesus, I thank You that we must come with empty hands. I thank You that You have done all – all – on the Cross, and that all we need in life or death is to be sure of this.'[8]

I have occasionally thought of something I would like to accomplish in the name of the Church – a book I'd like to write, hospitality to show church people, a desire I've asked for in prayer – and heard Jesus gently, seriously say: 'That's not

---

8   *The Hiding Place,* pp. 41-42.

something for me. That's something for you.' Sometimes our Christian to-do list is long with things we've added out of a sense of duty or ambition or personal desire, including some things which might be legitimate, but are not really there for Jesus' sake. We must be on our guard against such goals.

The place of good works

Susanna Wesley's life of Christian service proclaimed God's goodness and power to save, but it did not beg the question 'Should we then go on sinning?' as Paul does[9] – that God's grace is so limitless and extravagant that we are tempted to think our own obedience has no value at all. If we can add nothing to God's pleasure and joy in us, why bother living a Christian lifestyle?

But, of course, we are commanded to live lives of purity and fruitfulness. This is not to contribute to our salvation, or earn any additional favour from God, but to testify of Christ to the world by showing His character in us; to avoid bringing any shame on the name of Jesus; to grow more and more like Him for the sake of others, and closer and closer to Him for the sake of ourselves. When we have our eyes truly fixed on Jesus, how can we want to be anything other than like Him? He is so beautiful, so generous, so winsome, so joyful, so loving. We must desire to be like that so much that we are willing to undergo God's discipline and refining, often painful, to mould our character more and more like that of His Son. But to do so, we must keep our eyes not on ourselves

---

9   Romans 6:1.

– even on what God is doing through us – but raise them to Him, to His worship and praise and the awed contemplation of His character and sacrifice. May He give us the will to seek the Giver and not the gifts!

Repenting of our righteousness

What are the things you are most proud of in your Christian life – what personality traits, accomplishments or insights?

Of course, that is a trick question! Personal pride is always a trap for a Christian. If you're *proud* of that Bible study you led, prayer you said before the congregation or amount you raised for missions, don't let the Accuser tempt you into taking credit for them yourself. What is right and proper and glorious is to take *pleasure* in the things which Christ has done in you, and give Him thanks – but if you think you have time or resources or service to offer God as repayment for what He has done for you, you are in danger of taking Christ out of His proper place in your life.

Good works and ministry and Christian character are all vital for us, but not in the way we are tempted to think. Imagine that, after giving birth and raising a child for ten years, with all the sleeplessness, money, time and effort that involves, your child then came to you with a home-made card, made with pens and paper you had given him, and a crude but loving drawing of you and him on it. Your child says, 'I've been thinking about everything you've done for me, and I just made you this to say I love you.' You'd be thrilled with such thanks! But imagine he gives it to you and says, 'I spent ages on this. It's payment for all you've done for me!' ...Well, that's not only insufficient, it's downright insulting. It just highlights that your child has no real idea how much you've sacrificed for him. And as an illustration, this falls far short of what the Lord

When we start to feel really stressed about our Christian work, we have stopped trusting Christ to provide and preside over it. Whose work is it, anyway?!

has done for us, and how insufficient our small works are to 'repay' Him!

Be like the winsome child, looking around at the Lord's blessings, awed by them, eager just to return whatever thanks you can, knowing that God accepts humble and joyful gifts from His children.

The danger of focusing too much on our work – whether parenthood, ministry, church or career – is not only pride, but also losing focus on the reason for it. When we start to feel really stressed about our Christian work, we have stopped trusting Christ to provide and preside over it. Whose work is it, anyway?! We have taken the weight for His kingdom upon our own shoulders; and that is a recipe for worry, exhaustion and self-reliance. We start to resent our busyness and obligation. When we sense this starting to take hold, it is important to stop, rest, and spend some time dedicated just to seeking Jesus' company. The trouble, of course, is that this very busyness convinces us we don't have time or concentration for personal devotions! I've certainly been there. But there is really no other solution – not without God getting our attention in His own way. We must, at times, leave other things undone so that we can do the *most* important thing, just like Mary did when Martha was busy serving her houseful of people.

Scales from our eyes

Susanna Wesley was a woman saturated in biblical truth and theological understanding, with an outwardly upright life. If anyone had reason to boast, she more! Yet it was not in her power to see what was lacking – that sense of assurance, of the sufficiency of Christ. There are times when we can live a life that seeks Christ and still experience blind spots in our lives or faith. The opening of our eyes, the softening of our hearts, the bringing us to repentance and renewing our love of Jesus, all belong to the Lord. It is always His grace alone that works in us, that brings us closer to Himself. We can't accomplish that for ourselves; we struggle even to desire it for ourselves, especially when we are taking comfort elsewhere. It is God who reveals truth to us, who changes us, who gives us even the longing to draw near to Him.

And just as with Mrs Wesley, Communion is an opportune moment for this, especially when we take the time beforehand to truly meditate on His death and resurrection and examine our own hearts. Identifying with Christ, in this manner He has given us, is powerful. It shows up the ways in which we fall short, and it shows up His perfection and sacrifice and the cost of our salvation. It reminds us that Christ is in us, and we are in Him, and challenges us to root out the places where we are not abiding in the True Vine, where we have acted unworthy of His blood. Let's listen to the Communion table.

Can I bear fruit?

The good news of the Bible is that God can even use those He has rescued out of the pit of self-righteousness! There is such joy in humility. There is such joy in realising our freedom from our own accomplishments. There is such joy in repentance, opening our hearts to see Christ as we have never seen Him before.

What was missing in Susanna Wesley's example was so often winsomeness – that gentle, joyful spirit which attracts the world to a person and to the Lord she follows. A woman of great industry and efficiency may motivate us to follow her example, but it is less likely to attract us to her experience of Jesus. When we live in humility and reliance upon Christ – willing to change, ready to own up whenever we get it wrong, eager to tell people about Jesus' beauty and what He is doing in our hearts – that is when we become winsome Christians. That is when we direct glory to God. That is infinitely more fruitful than all the ministries we could ever run on our own strength.

Come to Him and rest, and bear fruit.

Questions

1. The famous hymn says, 'All to thee, my blessed Saviour, I surrender all.' Can you sing this hymn freely? Is there any area of your life you have not surrendered to the Lord?
2. Search your heart for your motivations in your acts of service. What things do you find stressful or obligatory, or do in order for others to notice?

3. Where in your life could you be more winsome and reflect Christ's character in such a way to draw others to Him?

Thou, O Christ, art all I want,
More than all in thee I find;
Raise the fallen, cheer the faint,
Heal the sick, and lead the blind.
Just and holy is thy name,
I am all unrighteousness;
False and full of sin I am;
Thou art full of truth and grace.
—'Jesus, Lover of My Soul', Charles Wesley, verse 3

10 The Fear of Man

Sarah Edwards

Sarah Pierpont was something of a spiritual prodigy – though, as a particularly humble girl, she would have been horrified by such a title. Born in Connecticut in 1710, her father was a minister and a founder of Yale University. From childhood she had intimate, almost visceral periods of communion with God, where she would be overcome with her thoughts of Christ, taking intense delight in His company for hours at a time.

At the age of thirteen, she met a Divinity student at her father's college called Jonathan Edwards. Jonathan was twenty, serious, and searching. He was impressed by Sarah's spiritual joy and openness. It was from her that he understood the possibility of man having not only knowledge of God, but a true relationship with Him. He also developed a respect for women as having as acute a spiritual experience as men, which was not the general view at that time!

When she was seventeen, Sarah married Jonathan, and they had eleven children together. She ran a home of great peace, discipline, happiness and generosity. There were, however, many hard circumstances, including the terrible pain of Jonathan's church turning against him over an issue of local politics. While God blessed his ministry throughout the American Colonies, including the powerful sermon *Sinners in the Hands of an Angry God,* Jonathan was often met with hostility in his own church and town. This was hard on both of the couple, and may have prompted Sarah's fixation on having people's good opinion and harmonious relationships.

Though Jonathan was industrious, devoted to Christ and theologically astute, he seemed to view Sarah as even closer to Christ than he was, with a deeper abiding in the Lord and an almost supernatural sense of the glory of heaven. Sarah had had many intense experiences of Christ, and had recently gone through a period of rededicating herself to Him – yet, in the winter of 1741, she found herself in spiritual darkness. Later, her husband took down Sarah's account of her crisis.

In Her Own Words

On Tuesday night, Jan. 19, 1742, I felt very uneasy and unhappy, at my being so low in grace. I thought I very much needed help from God, and found a spirit of earnestness to seek help of him, that I might have more holiness. When I had for a time been earnestly wrestling with God for it, I felt within myself great quietness of spirit, unusual submission to God, and willingness to wait upon him, with respect to the time and manner in which he should help me, and wished that he should take his own time, and his own way, to do it.

The next morning, I found a degree of uneasiness in my mind, at Mr. Edwards's suggesting, that he thought I had failed in some measure in point of prudence, in some conversation I had with Mr. Williams of Hadley, the day before. I found, that it seemed to bereave me of the quietness and calm of my mind, in any respect not to have the good opinion of my husband. This I much disliked in myself, as arguing a want of a sufficient rest in God, and felt a disposition to fight against it, and look to God for his help, that I might have a more full and entire rest in him, independent of all other things....

I had before this, so entirely given myself up to God, and resigned up everything into his hands, that I had, for a long time, felt myself quite alone in the world; so that the peace and calm of my mind, and my rest in God, as my only and all sufficient happiness, seemed sensibly above the reach of disturbance from any thing but these two: 1st. My own good name and fair reputation among men, and especially the esteem, and just treatment of the people of this town; 2dly. And more especially, the esteem, and love and kind treatment of my husband.[1]

Even though Sarah thought she had given every aspect of her life over to Christ, she became aware that the way she was perceived or favoured by others was still enough to disturb her walk with God.

---

1   All quotes from Sarah Edwards may be found at the following page: https://digital.library.upenn.edu/women/pierrepont/conversion/conversion.html. From Dwight, Sereno. *The Works of President Edwards: With a Memoir of His Life*. Vol. I. (New York: G. & C. & H. Carvill. 1830), pp. 171-190 (Chapter XIV). Sarah's husband, 'President Edwards', was one of the first presidents of Princeton University. Sereno Edwards Dwight was Jonathan Edwards' great-grandson.

After rebuking his wife in their conversation, Jonathan Edwards had to leave town to preach elsewhere. While Sarah was at family prayers later that morning, led by a friend, Mr Reynolds, she found herself longing that he would use the term *Father* in his prayer. Sarah asked herself if she could unreservedly call God her father, and she reached a new assurance that God looked not at her sins but instead at His Son, as she trusted in Him. Regardless of how other people saw her, her Father always looked upon her with a smile, as He did on His own Son, Jesus.

Sarah had in her mind Romans 8:34-35 (ESV), *Who is to condemn [us]? Christ Jesus is the one who died – more than that, who was raised – who is at the right hand of God, who indeed is interceding for us. Who shall separate us from the love of Christ?...*

She retreated to her room and read the whole chapter, which fell on her with an entirely new force.

> They appeared to me with undoubted certainty as the words of God, and as words which God did pronounce concerning me. I had no more doubt of it, than I had of my [own existence].... It appeared certain to me that God was my Father, and Christ my Lord and Savior, that he was mine and I his. Under a delightful sense of the immediate presence and love of God, these words seemed to come over and over in my mind, 'My God, my all; my God, my all'....
>
> After some time, the two evils mentioned above, as those which I should have been least able to bear, came to my mind – the ill treatment of the town, and the ill will of my husband – but now I was carried exceedingly above even such things

as these, and I could feel that, if I were exposed to them both, they would seem comparatively nothing.

For several days, Sarah continued to marvel in this greater realisation of Christ, His perfection, and His favour on her, with all earthly things receding from her view. But God was not only calling Sarah to repent of her fear of man – and receive freedom from it – but also of her pride on her husband's behalf. She was so jealous for Jonathan's glory that she hated seeing any visiting ministers meeting with greater success in the town than her husband.

> On Monday night...I had a deep and affecting impression, that the eye of God was ever upon my heart, and that it greatly concerned me to watch my heart, and see to it that I was perfectly resigned to God, with respect to the instruments he should make use of to revive religion in this town, and be entirely willing, if it was God's pleasure, that he should make use of [visiting minister] Mr. Buell...I was sensible what great cause I had to bless God, for the use he had made of Mr. Edwards hitherto; but thought, if he never blessed his labours any more, and should greatly bless the labours of other ministers, I could entirely acquiesce in his will...it was my instinctive feeling to say, 'Amen, Lord Jesus! Amen, Lord Jesus!' This seemed to be the sweet and instinctive language of my soul.

Indeed, Sarah prayed earnestly that God would bless the ministry of Mr Buell, and felt a sense from Him that her prayer would be answered, and revival would overtake the town. So it proved, almost immediately; there was a strong sense of God's presence and 'Christ's redeeming love' in the meetings over the next few days. Sarah found herself leaping out of her chair; unable to move for being overwhelmed by thoughts of Christ; and having a sense of being almost in heaven while she was half asleep. Though her dramatic experiences may sound intimidating, her renewed sense of God's pre-eminence and of her place before Him are entirely biblical and beautiful.

> God and Christ were so present to me, and so near me, that I seemed removed from myself. The spiritual beauty of the Father and the Saviour, seemed to engross my whole mind; and it was the instinctive feeling of my heart, 'Thou art; and there is none beside thee.' I never felt such an entire emptiness of self-love, or any regard to any private, selfish interest of my own. It seemed to me, that I had entirely done with myself. I felt that the opinions of the world concerning me were nothing, and that I had not more to do with any outward interest of my own, than with that of a person whom I never saw. The glory of God seemed to be all, and in all, and to swallow up every wish and desire of my heart.

> *For God gave us a spirit not of fear but of power and love and self-control.* (2 Tim. 1:7, ESV)

A Mystic or a Christian?

Wikipedia describes Sarah Edwards as a mystic. This is not a description I recognise of her, and not one I think she would recognise of herself. Sarah was an ordinary woman in whom God did extraordinary work. While she was sometimes affected by God's presence in unusual ways, these were not the kind of phenomena that we might associate as performative or spectacular; rather, she seemed to be simply filled with the joy of the Lord and realisation of His truth. She was not trying to start a new revival or movement or mode of worship – she was rather among the fruits of a revival that the Lord Himself was pouring out in the American colonies at that time. Above all, Sarah never tried to take attention for herself or win followers to her ways. Everything that she did was testament to Christ's glory and His work in her.

What is the Fear of Man?

The fear of man is a subtle burden, and we often overlook its more sinful aspects. There's nothing wrong with a desire to be respectable, liked, and amiable in society; there's nothing wrong with wanting a peaceful and conflict-free family. But how easily these things can become idols!

The desire to fit in can cause us to pass over opportunities to share the gospel. When faced with an opportunity, we wonder *what will they think of me?* Instead of *what will they think of Christ?* We overlook other people's true need of the Good News, looking instead at our own abilities and confidence and social acceptability. This reminds me particularly of Moses, who, ordered to go and begin the deliverance of God's people, was more worried about his fear of public speaking and looking like a fool in front of his old pals at the palace. We've all been Moses!

The desire to be part of contemporary culture leads us to overlook the profanity and impurity of the latest TV shows or music. It feels important to share the same gossip about actors, or know the same catchphrases, or be up-to-date on the same episode, even if we inwardly cringe at some of the content.

The cultural shibboleths of our time lead us to leave others' views unchallenged. We need to put in the hard mental work of thinking about our positions on issues like gay marriage, trans rights, and abortion. How do we show people compassion and openness without assenting to things that grieve the heart of God? This is particularly hard in these days of social media, where a trans-critical post from a decade ago can resurface and end a career, swallow a reputation.

We spoil our children or leave their bad behaviour unpunished in order to win their favour. Sometimes it just feels easier, doesn't it, to give in – avoid a row in the grocery store, leave that threat unfulfilled, buy a little silence

> *Sapphira illustrates an important characteristic of the fear of man – it often erodes our honesty.*

with a few chocolate buttons rather than buckling in for the hard, Susanna Wesley-style parenting that sets good boundaries and patterns.

We nurse a hurt or grievance in silence rather than expose ourselves to criticism or conflict from a spouse or friend. Pretending an issue doesn't exist seems much safer than risking a bitter rift or, worse, having our own faults exposed as well as our friend's. There are also times when we are simply afraid of someone's reaction and we'd rather not kick that hornet's nest. I often wonder if that is what happened with Ananias and Sapphira, who lied to the elders of the church about what proportion of income they were tithing. Did Sapphira lie out of a desire to look good to the church, like her husband, or was she backing up his story to maintain peace in her home? Either way, she put other people's opinions of

> *If we change ourselves to win favour from others, rather than letting Christ change us to be more like Himself, then we put on a lie.*

her ahead of God's, and it cost her her life.

Sapphira illustrates an important characteristic of the fear of man – it often erodes our honesty. It nudges us to present a false image to the world. If we don't think we're cool enough, we'll show off and avoid exposing our vulnerabilities. If we want to look kinder than we really are, we'll serve others but with resentment in our hearts. If we are conflict-avoiders, then anger and pain will fester underneath our every encounter with 'that person' – and they might not even be aware of it. These things are pernicious. If we change ourselves to win favour from others, rather than letting Christ change us to be more like Himself, then we put on a lie.[2]

All of these things see relationships and social acceptance as more important to our peace of mind than obedience to God. It should not be the case that other people's opinions of us so cloud our emotions as to take away our peace in the Lord. Of course, we are social souls – created as such to reflect the fellowship of the Trinity – so it does not come naturally to us to disregard the opinions of the people around us. Nor should we wear the attitude of 'I don't care what anyone thinks!' in

---

2   https://www.desiringgod.org/articles/for-better-or-worse (Accessed September 2021)

the cold, hard, defiant sense. Rather, Sarah Edwards shows us how our standing before the Lord can simply outshine our other relationships.

All eyes on Jesus

Sarah's spiritual revelation originated in a sense of discouragement from her husband's rebuke, but her experience moved very quickly from seeking the Lord's comfort to seeking the *Lord Himself.* He answered her unspoken question in a way that she had not anticipated. Sarah must have questioned in prayer whether or not she had acted properly; whether her husband had spoken to her kindly; how to 'do better'; whether she was really acceptable before God. But Christ's response was not to answer these questions. It was to assure her that He Himself *was* the answer. His justification, His peace, His glory, His person.

> *Do you want to see a change in your character, home or community? Spend time seeking Jesus*

How often do we seek change in our lives, or in others' lives, rather than seeking Jesus Himself? How often do we seek His blessings rather than His company? His mere help, rather than His own mighty, living strength? We invite Him to work in our lives, while really keeping our focus upon ourselves. Yet, when we truly look to Jesus and meditate upon Him, trusting Him to do what is best, that is when He does His work in us. We strive to change ourselves into something *we* find acceptable, forgetting that acceptance is His gift already bestowed upon us.

Let's look for Jesus, learn from Him, adore Him; and as our hearts become filled up with Himself, He inevitably changes us. Our priorities, reactions, habits and speech – none of these remain untouched as we simply walk alongside Him, basking in His presence. Do you want to see a change in your character, home or community? Spend time seeking Jesus. His transforming work in you will soon be reflected not only in your attitudes toward your situation, but in your situation itself as you start to respond with Christ's character. Instead of putting on a lie, follow the instruction of Romans 13:14 (ESV) to 'put on the Lord Jesus Christ'.

> *...your own sin of fear (which is a lack of trust in the Lord) is not 'better' than their sins toward you*

Making a start

Finding freedom in our Christian lives often follows a scriptural pattern. First, we are convicted of our own sin and the hopelessness of that sin. Now, you may be battered by life – slandered, abused, neglected, mocked or bullied by those around you. But if you have let fear dictate your responses to those people, you need to recognise that your own sin of fear (which is a lack of trust in the Lord) is not 'better' than their sins toward you. We are used to thinking of fear as a burden, not a sin. And the Lord does have compassion on the fearful. But, when you avoid conflict through fear, you fail to love people well, by enabling their sin to flourish. When you avoid speaking of Christ because of how others might look down on you, you pass up an opportunity to offer them the truth and security they need. When you dress provocatively or blur ethical lines at work to fit in with those around you, you weaken your Christian

ensure that you are listening to the Judge and not the Accuser

witness and lead others into temptation. Fear is a thing that doesn't just affect your life, but those around you as well. The Bible tells us hundreds of times not to be afraid, and these are words of both assurance and conviction; we *must* not fear, but at the same time, we *need* not fear.

Let's look with open eyes at our own failings. BUT, ensure that you are listening to the Judge and not the Accuser. How do you tell the difference? In my experience, the Accuser sounds like a bully. A name-caller. A threatener. The Accuser insists: 'You're an enabler. You'll never have the courage to break out of this pattern. You're just weak.' 'Yes, you do look cheap. In fact, you *are* cheap. You look good but you're not worth very much inside.' 'You've gone too far. Change is too hard now.' 'Look how you could have talked about Jesus there, and you failed again! You should just accept that you'll always fail. I guess evangelism just isn't your gift.'

The Judge says, 'Your heart needs to change. You need me. My Son has paid for your sin; are you willing to die to it, as He died for you, and be set free?'

The language of the Judge is perfectly expressed in the look which Jesus turned upon Peter after his thrice-denial of Christ: a look of sorrowful but loving reproach, which rebukes but offers restoration at the same time. Looking at your sin is important – in the book of James we are urged to grieve and wail over it – but conviction only takes you so far. Repentance, looking to Him who paid for your sin so you might be 'accepted in the Beloved', should take up far more of our time.

Finding Freedom

When you've been in a sinful attitude or pattern for a long time – even as a saved person, and even while striving against it – it becomes hard to imagine freedom. You may recall that Christie Dondero Bettwy, in our chapter about eating disorders, heard about freedom from food anxiety and wondered 'Is it even possible for a woman to live like that?'

Freedom from fear is possible, and I know that because it's one of my most insidious spiritual issues. Here is what I've found helpful.

1. When you repent, really let the Lord root out all the sin, all the causes behind it; and make changes to your lifestyle that will open your whole heart more to Him. What have you not surrendered? This is important because sin is never a one-issue problem in our hearts. It infects *everything*, and *everything* is related. All habitual sin must be laid bare and offered up before Christ.

2. Fasting helps. Different people have different reasons for fasting. Mine is that a hunger pang points me back to Christ: reminds me of His nearness, reminds me of His sufficiency to do all things for me. This need not be for a whole day or from all foods, but any form of self-denial and breaking of our usual habits for a short time points us back to Jesus: the one true need. I have sometimes fasted

on a day when I knew I was going to be anxious about something, and was amazed how that constant prayer lifted the burden of fear.

3. Eat Scripture. Write down a few verses that genuinely strengthen and comfort you, and feed on them throughout the day. Write them on your hand or memorise them. Listen to a helpful preacher or Bible study as you go about your day, or to Christian music. It lifts your mind off your own worries.

4. Praise. Even when you don't feel like it. Even when all you can think of to praise about is 'You are God. I don't feel the goodness but I know the goodness. You are good.' Praying the Psalms is a fantastic way to do this.

5. Repeat daily. I can't stress the importance of this enough. Our emotions will surely ebb and flow, and spiritual discipline is not a formula for good vibes. Yet, we must be persistent in laying our weakness before the Lord every day, asking Him to work in us every day, asking Him to control what we can't control, asking Him for His nearness and His gift of 'power and love and a sound mind'. If we lose that sense of needing Him, we stop abiding, and the fear roars back as soon as our situation veers out of our control.

Can I bear fruit?

If you fulfil all of these steps – frequent repentance, meditating on Scriptures, praise, daily abiding – you will bear fruit. Sometimes you still have to wait to see it. But it's a promise, not from me, but from the Saviour. 'Whoever abides in me, and I in him, he it is that bears much fruit' (John 15:5, ESV). Fear is debilitating. We can't conquer it on our own. We can't reason our way out of it, run away from it, or outgrow it. But happily, we know someone who can.

The Overcomer

I end the book with this chapter because of the one absolutely delightful truth that it encapsulates.

We are not the ones who overcome. **Jesus has overcome.** He has been in every respect tempted as we are, yet without sin;[3] He was obedient to the point of death, even death on a cross;[4] He is seated on the right hand of God;[5] He is coming again to receive His people to Himself.[6]

Yet we who have entered into the covenant of Jesus' blood are so much His own that we are dead to sin, even as He is; dead to reproach (fear of man) even as He is; dead to death. We look forward to being glorified and reigning with Him, because we are in Him, and He is in us. Can we ever grasp that truth? We memorise it and speak it, but can we really understand that the great I Am, the Creator, the Lamb, the one perfect Son of God, makes us so clean and so new that we are dead to ourselves and live only in Him? When we are conscious of our abiding in Him, fear melts away into insignificance, leaving us with wonder and awe and delight in

---

3 Hebrews 4:15.

4 Philippians 2:8.

5 Colossians 3:1.

6 1 Thess. 4:16-18.

our Saviour. Through Him, we overcome all things. O come, let us adore Him!

Sarah Edwards did not 'achieve' a greater enlightenment in God, as the term Mystic might suggest. She was not better or holier clay than we are. She struggled with sin; and the fear of man is not a light sin, but can cripple our spiritual life. Christ reached down into her weakness and gave her an overwhelming sense of His grace. It is always Him who changes us. Always Him who gives us even the will and the openness to repent. Always Him who gives us His strength, His sufficiency. He opens our eyes and our hearts. He heals us of our illnesses and fills our loneliness.[7] He calls us by name.[8] He keeps on working in us until we are completed in Him.[9] He holds on to us when we are weak – holds us like babies, no matter how old we get.[10] It is always Him who delivers. We think we are seeking Him, but all along it was always Him who sought and rescued us.[11] We are part of His story, not He part of ours. And in Him, we live and move and have our being.[12] All glory be to Christ!

How can we fear? To Him belongs the honour we wish to find in our communities and churches, the peace we long for in our hearts when others hurt us. He can indeed move and soften the hearts of those who have done us wrong, but they

---

7   Psalm 103.

8   John 10:3.

9   Philippians 1:6.

10   Isaiah 46:4.

11   1 John 4:19; Romans 5:8.

12   Acts 17:28.

need this **no more than we do.** Let us seek Him for their sake, let us seek Him for our sake, but most of all, let us seek Him for His own sake.

Questions

1. What are some fears and insecurities you bear towards other people? To what extent do you think they are burdens or sins?

2. What does it look like to 'put on the Lord Jesus Christ'? If we are clothed in Him, how does that help us to leave fear behind and react to people differently?

3. What are some ways Jesus has 'overcome' in your life? What are some other areas where you long to see Him win the victory over an issue?

Our sins they are many, his mercy is more.
Praise the Lord, his mercy is more!
Stronger than darkness, new every morn,
Our sins they are many, his mercy is more.
—'His Mercy is More', Matt Boswell and Matt Papa

Afterword

At the start of the year in which I wrote this book, I had a sense of what God wanted to teach me: that what was impossible with me was possible with Him. I had to stop striving and start trusting! I thought at that time that I would see Him change circumstances over which I felt helpless. In fact, He has spent this year changing me: giving me a clearer view of my own sin, of my need of Him, and of His beauty. This has been a lesson through desert and fire and gnawing anxiety (2020, eh?). But He has given me a greater measure of spiritual life than ever before.

A confession: when I agreed to write this book, I did so as a measure of prudence, perhaps even pride – despite hating research, I thought it was a good career move! In fact, God has used the examples of these wonderful, redeemed sisters to challenge and inspire much change in my heart and my life. Now I come to my research and my computer wondering what truths about Himself He will reveal today.

God still has a lot of work to do in me! I am sometimes downcast by how much there is yet to overcome so that

I might find the obedience of Rosaria Butterfield, the uncompromising truthfulness of Doreen Virtue, or the freedom of Sarah Edwards. But, dear sister, I know that He who began a good work in us will see it through to the day of completion, if we lay our hearts willing and bare before Him. I pray that you will enter into His strength and grace and joy, and I would have you pray the same for me, to His glory!

As is fitting in this book for women, I have several women to thank.

From the outset I found inspiration, loving support and excellent ideas from my friend Edie Overduin, a brilliant researcher and woman of God.

My editor, Rosanna Burton, kept me going when I wondered, through lockdown and faltering concentration, if I would ever finish writing it!

And I never would have, if not for my wonderful mother-in-law, Catriona MacLeod, who provided a whole book's worth of free babysitting.

My mother, Janet Devan, gave me excellent critique and, of course, made this book much better.

Anne Norrie, my 'details' editor, really met me in the nuts and bolts of the book, going through each chapter offering helpful advice and encouragement.

I am thankful to all those who contributed or agreed for me to include their stories: Dr Rosaria Butterfield, Christie Dondero Bettwy, Emma Scrivener, MC Rios, Catriona Murray, and Doreen Virtue.

Please feel free to get in touch with me via my blog, mostreliable.wordpress.com

Resources

Chapter 1

Butterfield, Rosaria Champagne, *Openness Unhindered: Further Thoughts of an Unlikely Convert on Sexual Identity and Union with Christ* (Pittsburgh, Pennsylvania: Crown & Covenant Publications, 2015). This is a truly fascinating book for anyone interested in queer theory and its intersection with Christianity, or indeed on the subject of identity in Christ regardless of sexual background.

Butterfield, Rosaria Champagne, *The Secret Thoughts of an Unlikely Convert: An English Professor's Journey into Christian Faith* (Pittsburgh, Pennsylvania: Crown & Covenant Publications, 2012). An important autobiography, elegant and academic, yet suffused with humility. Compulsive reading.

Chapter 2

King, Don. (Ed.) *Out of My Bone: the Letters of Joy Davidman* (Grand Rapids, MI: Eerdmans, 2009). Joy's letters are lively and paint a picture of a difficult, intelligent, brilliant woman, often weak, but who found power to change through Christ breaking through.

Lewis, C.S. *A Grief Observed* (London: Faber & Faber, 1961). Philosophy, theology and love-letter meet in this heart-rending account of Joy's death and Jack's mourning.

Vernick, Leslie. *The Emotionally Destructive Marriage: How to Find Your Voice and Reclaim Your Hope* (Colorado Springs, CO: Waterbrook/Multnomah, 2013). A watershed book on helping women in emotionally abusive marriages look at the situation objectively and find courage and wisdom to make a change.

Chapter 3

Elliot, Elisabeth, *Through Gates of Splendour* (Milton Keynes, UK: Authentic Media edition 2005, first printed 1956). A powerful and page-turning account of adventure, evangelism and grief.

Elliot, Elisabeth, *A Path Through Suffering* (Grand Rapids, MI: Revell, 2014). First published by Servant Publications in 1990. A beautiful meditation and apologetic on the 'why' of grief and the God who walks through it with us.

Kayleneyoder.com – Kaylene's blog has been an important resource in my spiritual life. Her prayers in particular are deeply scriptural and a valuable aid when you wish to deepen your prayer life.

Posttenebraslux.co.uk – Catriona Murray, a lecturer and public servant, writes elegantly, powerfully and honestly about widowhood, church life, and lessons drawn from her life in the Hebridean Isles of Scotland.

Chapters 4 & 5

ten Boom, Corrie, *The Hiding Place* (London: Hodder & Stoughton, 1972). This classic of Christian literature bears many readings – it's both exciting and fearful, introduces the reader to a whole cast of new friends, and always encourages one in endurance, forgiveness, sacrifice, adoration of the Lord, and so much more. There is such a sufficiency of teaching in this one short book that it could fill more than these two chapters!

Chapter 6

joyfulandexpectant.wordpress.com – Christie Dondero Bettwy's blog is honest, useful and warm. It's a great place to start for anyone who needs to hear the truth that 'freedom is possible'.

Rock Recovery Trust: https://rockrecoveryed.org. This organisation, which Christie runs and represents, plugs gaps in support for overcoming eating disorders. Currently operating in the US, their website is a useful starting place for anyone in finding help.

Scrivener, Emma, *A New Name: Grace and Healing for Anorexia* (London: IVP, 2012). Emma also blogs at emmascrivener. net. I simply cannot recommend this book highly enough – it informed my understanding of eating disorders, and of my loved ones who suffer with them, more than I can say.

Chapter 7

Rhodes Jr., Ray, *Susie: The Life and Legacy of Susannah Spurgeon, Wife of Charles H. Spurgeon* (Chicago, IL: Moody Publishers, 2018). This is a warm, loving account that feels like pulling up a seat at the fire and talking to a friend. Susie was full of God's wisdom and grace, and Ray Rhodes does a wonderful job of making it all accessible and engaging.

I would also point readers toward Irene Howat's *Pain, My Companion* (Ross-shire: Christian Focus Publications, 1970). A classic of Christian growth, patience and fortitude along a difficult path made sweet by the Lord's presence.

Chapter 8

Virtue, Doreen, *Deceived No More: How Jesus Led Me Out of the New Age and Into His Word* (Nashville, TN: Emanate Books, 2020). Website: doreenvirtue.com. Doreen provides a wealth of anti-falsehood information, testimony, scriptural analysis, and most of all, a living, uncompromising witness to the truth of the Bible and how it shapes our lives.

Shalomaz.com: The House of New Beginnings, a Messianic church based in Arizona, gives excellent Bible teaching online every day. Rabbi Cosmo Panzetta's teaching is a counter-cultural, fresh, grace-filled challenge on how to live Christ's way in a dark world. https://www.youtube.com/watch?v=YjUYYv0LqIU: 'Designer Thoughts' sermon, dealing with temptation and false beliefs.

John Bunyan's *Pilgrim's Progress* can be found here for free:

http://www.covenantofgrace.com/pilgrims_progress.htm
It is also possible to buy copies in more modern language, or
even as a film! Whichever way you take in the story (I have
fond memories of an illustrated children's book), the vivid
picture of Pilgrim, his friends and his battles stay with you for
a lifetime.

Chapter 9
Dallimore, Arnold, *Susanna Wesley: The Mother of John &
Charles Wesley* (Ada, MI: Baker Books, 1993). This is an
intimate portrait of a complex woman: at times intimidating,
but impossible not to respect and seek to emulate. The Wesleys
had a dramatic family life, between a turbulent marriage, an
unwed pregnancy, multiple devastating house fires, and even a
'haunting'. An absolutely fascinating read whether or not you
have already encountered John and Charles Wesley!

Chapter 10
Sarah Edwards' firsthand account of her personal revival
can be found at https://digital.library.upenn.edu/women/
pierrepont/conversion/conversion.html. From Dwight,
Sereno, *The Works of President Edwards: With a Memoir of His
Life*, Vol. I. (New York: G. & C. & H. Carvill, 1830). pp. 171-
190 [Chapter XIV]. Of all the women in this book, Sarah's
experience is the one I have most coveted for myself. While
the whole of her story is written in 'King James' language, it's a
deeply rewarding effort to see how her love of Christ eclipsed
everything in her life.

Christian Focus Publications

Our mission statement —

STAYING FAITHFUL

In dependence upon God we seek to impact the world through literature faithful to His infallible Word, the Bible. Our aim is to ensure that the Lord Jesus Christ is presented as the only hope to obtain forgiveness of sin, live a useful life and look forward to heaven with Him.

Our books are published in four imprints:

CHRISTIAN
FOCUS

Popular works including biographies, commentaries, basic doctrine and Christian living.

CHRISTIAN
HERITAGE

Books representing some of the best material from the rich heritage of the church.

MENTOR

Books written at a level suitable for Bible College and seminary students, pastors, and other serious readers. The imprint includes commentaries, doctrinal studies, examination of current issues and church history.

CF4•K

Children's books for quality Bible teaching and for all age groups: Sunday school curriculum, puzzle and activity books; personal and family devotional titles, biographies and inspirational stories — because you are never too young to know Jesus!

Christian Focus Publications Ltd,
Geanies House, Fearn, Ross-shire,
IV20 1TW, Scotland, United Kingdom.
www.christianfocus.com